GOD
IS JUST
NOT
FAIR

Finding Hope When Life Doesn't Make Sense

JENNIFER ROTHSCHILD

Praise for *God Is Just Not Fair*

Like David, Job, Jeremiah, and other saints of old, Jennifer Rothschild asks the hard questions of God with startling honesty and refreshing transparency. And, akin to Jacob, Jennifer wrestles mightily with God through the dark night of her soul—that readers might experience the relief of His light and the certain assurance of His blessings.

> Ann Voskamp, author of the *New York Times* bestseller
> *One Thousand Gifts: A Dare to Live Fully Right Where You Are*

In this tender book full of compassion, Jennifer wrestles through the questions that can rise to the surface during painful circumstances. "Why is this happening?" "Is God there and does He care?" Unlike other resources that wrestle with these deep issues from the head, Jennifer does so from the heart. She will show you how to have unrelenting courage to plead for God's power and, at the same time, for remarkable strength to trust God's plan. This is a book I'll be recommending for years to come.

> Lysa TerKeurst, *New York Times* bestselling author
> and president of Proverbs 31 Ministries

Why does God allow bad things to happen to good people? This is the faith-wrecking question asked by believers and atheists alike. It has caused millions of the faithful to doubt everything they thought they knew about God. Jennifer Rothschild speaks to this issue like few others—offering real answers with refreshing personal insights, solid biblical truth, and genuine heartfelt compassion. She can speak to you because she's been there and she cares. If your life isn't making sense, read *God is Just Not Fair*, and discover how God is using your trials to lead you to hope, healing, and joy.

> Kirk Cameron, television and film actor

What Jennifer teaches us is rooted and grounded in truth. What is truth? It's God's Word which sets us apart and enables us to live in the courage of faith. How this is exemplified in my precious friend's life! I am so proud of you, Jennifer, for taking us to the bread of life and nourishing our souls.

> Kay Arthur, cofounder of Precept Ministries International,
> focused on the mission of establishing people in God's Word

After many years of great friendship and Bible study with Jennifer Rothschild, I have witnessed her immense passion for Christ's ability to heal and inspire others. In *God Is Just Not Fair*, she asks the hardest, timeless questions of faith while bringing hope to others who, like Jennifer, have gone through the testing challenges of life.

Mark Richt, head football coach, University of Georgia

At some point in our lives, I am betting that every one of us has cried out, "Why, God?" My friend Jennifer understands that heart cry at the deepest level—and has a lifetime of wisdom to share with us. *God Is Just Not Fair* is a wonderful, wonderful book. Jennifer does not settle for pat, easy answers but encourages us to ask the hard questions and then hold tight to the eternal perspective that is the only way the answers will truly be found.

Shaunti Feldhahn, social researcher and bestselling author
of *For Women Only.*

"God, is this fair?" My wife and I asked this question after the passing of our precious daughter. The fact is, everything in life doesn't turn out the way we expect—just ask Jennifer Rothschild, one of our favorite LIFE Today guests who became blind as a fifteen-year-old. With candor, Jennifer deals head-on with deep, probing questions many of us have asked. For those who wonder if God hears their prayers ... cares ... or even if *God is good*, this book will point you to Hope. Ultimately, "what matters most is not the questions," Jennifer writes, "but the heart of the questioner."

James Robison, founder, LIFE Outreach International,
cohost, "LIFE Today" Television, Fort Worth, Texas

GOD
IS JUST
NOT
FAIR

Also by Jennifer Rothschild

Fingerprints of God

Fresh Grounded Faith:
Devotions to Awaken Your Spirit

Lessons I Learned in the Dark:
Steps to Walking by Faith, Not by Sight

Self Talk, Soul Talk:
What to Say When You Talk to Yourself

GOD IS JUST NOT FAIR

Finding Hope When Life Doesn't Make Sense

JENNIFER ROTHSCHILD

ZONDERVAN

God Is Just Not Fair
Copyright © 2013 by Jennifer Rothschild

This title is also available as a Zondervan ebook. Visit www.zondervan.com/ebooks.

Requests for information should be addressed to:
Zondervan, 3900 *Sparks Dr., Grand Rapids, Michigan 49546*

Library of Congress Cataloging-in-Publication Data

Rothschild, Jennifer.
    God is just not fair : finding hope when life doesn't make sense / Jennifer Rothschild.—
First [edition]
       p.   cm.
    ISBN 978-0-310-33858-1 (softcover)
      1. Providence and government of God—Christianity. 2. Suffering—Religious aspects—
Christianity. 3. Consolation. I. Title.
    BT135.R77 2014
    248.8'6—dc23   2013032617

Interior design and composition: Greg Johnson/Textbook Perfect

Printed in the United States of America

14 15 16 17 18 19 /DCI/ 22 21 20 19 18 17 16 15 14 13 12 11 10 9 8 7 6 5 4 3 2 1

CONTENTS

INTRODUCTION: What I Didn't Want You to Know   **11**

PART 1: God, Are You Fair?   **17**

1. Just Desserts   21
2. Divine Inequality   31
3. Justice Delayed, Justice Denied   37
4. Stark Raving Grateful   44

PART 2: God, Do You Err?   **53**

5. Wrestling with God's Ways   57
6. Perfectly Strange   65
7. Can the Immutable Change?   72
8. Not the God We Expect   78

PART 3: God, Do You Hear Prayer?   **85**

9. Can You Even Hear Me?   87
10. God, If You're Listening, Make a Move!   95
11. Good God, Lousy Answers   102
12. The Ultimate Answer   107
13. Jesus Had an Unanswered Prayer Too   112

PART 4: God, Do You Care?   **119**

14. Compassionate Inactivity   121
15. Where There's Ability, There's Responsibility   130
16. If You Care, Get Me Out of Here   140
17. Spectator Grace   148
18. You Will Be OK   154

PART 5: God, Are You Aware?   **159**

19. God Only Knows   161
20. He Knows Your Name   169
21. His Eye Is on You   173
22. Tell God What He Already Knows   178
23. Forgetful Omniscience   183
24. God, Am I Aware?   188

PART 6: God, Are You There?   **195**

   25. AWOL   197
   26. Hide-and-Seek   202
   27. If You Had Been Here   208
   28. Bethel for Your Soul   213
   29. He Travels with You on Your Road   217
   30. Keep Walking Toward Him   224

CONCLUSION: What I Really Want You to Know   **232**

ACKNOWLEDGMENTS   237

I know now, Lord, why you utter no answer. You are yourself the answer. Before your face questions die away. What other answer would suffice?

C. S. Lewis, *Till We Have Faces*

What I Didn't Want You to Know

Let us step into the darkness and reach out for the hand of God.
The path of faith and darkness is so much safer than the one we
would choose by sight.

George MacDonald

Have you heard all the right answers when it comes to faith?
If you have, do those answers always feel right? Does everything about your faith make sense to you? Or, like me, do you sometimes have questions about God and his ways?

There are hard things in our lives that don't make sense and
invite so many questions. Questions like these:

If God is good, why do we suffer?

Why are innocent children treated unjustly?

Why doesn't God heal when he is capable?

When difficulty, tragedy, or crisis occurs, questions about God
inevitably arise.

When you see injustice in the world, innocent children suffering … *God, is this fair?*

When tragedy strikes and nothing in your life seems to make
sense … *God, do you err?*

When you ask God year after year to help you lose weight,
be more patient, overcome your temper … *God, do you hear my*
prayer?

When a spouse leaves … *God, do you care?*

When you get a pink slip instead of a paycheck ... *God, are you aware?*

When you wonder if you will ever stop feeling lonely because you long for a baby, a spouse, a friend ... *God, are you there?*

When rough things happen to us, it's as if they rip holes in the fabric of our faith, or what I sometimes call our "blanket of faith."

The Blanket of Faith

We all have a blanket of faith. It's woven together from the strands of what we believe about God and what we have experienced in our relationship with him. We wrap ourselves in this blanket and it helps us to feel protected and comforted. Some of us have well-worn blankets of faith because we have walked with God for years and years. I do. My blanket of faith is over forty years old! Others of us may have a brand-new blanket of faith, and we're still learning how to wrap ourselves in it. But no matter how long we've had our blanket of faith, we all feel more secure when we're wrapped in it.

But then life happens.

Rip.

And it tears a big hole in our blanket of faith. We feel exposed and insecure. We wonder if our faith will really be enough to protect and comfort us. Every heartache we endure raises difficult questions, and each question has the potential to tear a new hole in our blanket of faith. The very faith we had hoped would shelter and comfort us suddenly feels inadequate and leaves us feeling even more vulnerable to the harsh winds of sorrow and fear.

Can you relate? I bet you can. Most of us will readily admit we've experienced some confusing circumstances, asked some tough questions, and wondered, *Is God fair?* We all have some holes in our faith blankets. I can guess you might have one you're dealing with right now because you picked up this book. Well, my friend, I have *lived* the questions in this book, and you should have seen my blanket of faith not too long ago. It was a tattered mess. And, to be honest, I was terrified because the one thing I had depended on—my faith—had been reduced to rags, and I was needy, vulnerable, and afraid without it.

Torn Up

It was about five years ago, and I was in the midst of a rough year full of questions, discontent, and depression. I was still traveling the country, teaching the Bible, and speaking of God's peace and goodness, but privately I was battling despair. My comforting blanket of faith was deteriorating, and my lifelong assumptions about God— the foundations of my faith—were being shaken and shattered.

During this difficult season, I kept a diary of my spiritual journey—a diary I certainly didn't want you or anyone else to read! This snapshot of my life was private, and it definitely wasn't what someone who read "books by Jennifer Rothschild" would expect to read. Here is a brief glimpse of what I couldn't tell anyone at the time:

> My faith is really being tested, and I am failing. I am questioning so much about God—who he is, where he is, even *if* he is.
>
> I don't know the answers. None of us really, really know. We just believe and hope. I have waded through this agony all week and wondered why I am feeling and thinking this way. Perhaps it's just another affirmation that I am spiritually blind. I cannot see God unless he opens my eyes and allows me to see him. I have seen images of the God I thought I knew through Bible study, Christian platitudes, and Sunday school lessons. But the God I am learning about now is so beyond my comprehension that I have grappled with the notion that he isn't even real. This confusion makes no sense.
>
> *God, please give me the peace I once had. I don't want peace that comes from intentional ignorance. I want peace that comes from you. Peace that is unexplainable. Peace that can afford to question but exist without answers.*

See what I mean? My blanket of faith was in tatters. It's hard to even revisit those feelings and thoughts now because they were so painful. I was deeply afraid of how insecure the questions made me feel. I felt unmoored from what I thought I knew about God, and I was afraid to say it out loud to anyone because then it would feel even more real. But it was the real, raw, and radically honest truth about what I was going through—and I couldn't have written the pages of this book without first living through those difficult questions.

Have you ever had such difficult feelings or tried to make sense of your faith, only to end up with more questions? Have you tried to wrap yourself in a blanket of faith and realized there were so many holes in it that it no longer protected or comforted you? Maybe you're there right now, and that's why you picked up this book.

If that's the case, know you are not alone.

People of faith have been asking tough questions for millennia. The technical term for the problem of suffering is "theodicy." The word itself has its roots in the Greek words for God (*theos*) and justice (*dikē*). It was coined in the seventeenth century by one of the greatest thinkers of the Enlightenment period, Gottfried Wilhelm Leibniz. Theodicy attempts to explain how and why there can be evil and suffering in the world if God is powerful and good.

Theodicy is a "head" term, but its implications are "heart" issues. So, rather than being an intellectual pursuit of theodicy, this book is a heart pursuit. The head pursues answers; our hearts need more than answers—we need comfort. We need to know that God cares and is aware of our suffering. We need to feel his empathy when we are entwined in a painful mystery of faith. We need to feel that our blanket of faith can protect us; that the holes can be filled with answers. That's where I was in 2009. I desperately needed his reassurance—I needed to know that he was there, that he was good, and that he was just. And actually, I am still there! Even though I feel more comfortable with the questions, the answers aren't what ultimately got me through. Answers are not what mend the holes in our blankets of faith. Answers are not what will get you through your tough times either. But, my friend, you should still ask the questions.

Mending the Blanket of Faith

Job is perhaps the best-known biblical figure to wrestle with the questions of faith that come from great suffering. Here are some of Job's questions:

- Why did I not perish at birth, and die as I came from the womb? (Job 3:11)
- Why is light given to those in misery, and life to the bitter of soul? (Job 3:20)
- Why do you hide your face and consider me your enemy? (Job 13:24)
- Why do the wicked live on, growing old and increasing in power? (Job 21:7)

And these are only a few of the more than sixty questions recorded in the book of Job!

Interestingly, Job also wrote, "Though he slay me, yet will I hope in him ... I know that my redeemer lives" (Job 13:15; 19:25). Standing in the rubble of his life, wrapped in a tattered blanket of faith, with far more questions than answers, Job said he knew that God lived? He said that no matter what God did, he would still hope in him? How could Job have that kind of peace? How could he hold on to that conviction in the face of so much unfairness and loss in his life? How could he feel secure in his relationship with God when God hadn't fixed his situation or provided answers to fill in the missing pieces in his blanket of faith?

The answer to all those questions is, simply, God.

It was not what God did, what God didn't do, what God said, or how God answered that gave Job such peace and contentment. It was because he encountered God in the ashes of his life. Job continued to wrap himself in his blanket of faith, no matter how torn and tattered it was. And Job was able to experience the comfort and strength he needed because God *did* fill in all the broken places; he filled in each and every hole with himself.

My friend, that's what he does for you and me too. God doesn't fill the holes in our blankets of faith with answers or solutions. He fills the holes in our blanket of faith with himself. Philosophy, intellectual answers, or religion alone will never be enough to repair the holes in your faith. Only God can fill the missing pieces.

And he fills them with himself.

Do you want that? I sure do.

As you travel with me through the pages of this book, my prayer is that you will experience an encounter with God as we wrestle with tough questions. When we are totally satisfied by a relationship with God, answers won't seem as important to us.

I know you may not only "ask" questions; I know you probably have "lived" the questions. I understand. I have lived the tough questions too — as a teenager who lost her sight; as a middle-aged woman who fell into a debilitating depression, and as a woman who loved God and believed in him and yet struggled with unbelief. God became the one answer for me and gave me emotional stability, hope, and comfort. My blanket of faith was ultimately strengthened by my doubts; it became even more comforting and strong because of how God filled in my many missing pieces. I want you to experience the same comfort and hope.

Though this book will thoughtfully and honestly grapple with six big questions of faith, what matters most is not the questions but the heart of the questioner. By the end of this book, I pray you will realize that seeking to know answers is far less important than seeking to know God.

So wrap yourself in your blanket of faith — no matter how new or old it is, no matter how torn or strong it is. Feel it surround you and comfort you as you examine the holes that may be in it. Give yourself permission to ask questions to God. He will often reveal the answer. But far more importantly, invite him to reveal himself to you in the midst of your questions.

He will come to you. He will fill all the holes in your blanket of faith with peace, love, grace, and strength. For he *is* Peace, Love, Grace, and Strength.

Jennifer Rothschild

PART 1

God, Are You Fair?

It was an ordinary July day in a Tallahassee movie theater during the cheap movie series—at least that's what I used to call it. Our local theater featured cartoon movies during the summer for just $2—and that price included the popcorn. On a Wednesday morning, I got three-year-old Clayton dressed, packed the diaper bag, and slipped my Walkman cassette player (yes, this was before CDs) into my purse. This was the third movie in the series, and I had finally figured out how to entertain myself during the ninety minutes of cartoon silliness.

I grabbed a message tape someone had given me many years earlier. I had never listened to it because even though I was curious about it, I also dreaded it. I knew the woman's story, and it was both similar to and different from my own. I was afraid to hear it, to feel it, and then to have to deal with it.

I have never enjoyed going into dark movie theaters because they are so difficult for me to get around in. But on this day it wasn't so bad because I had my friend Becky as my guide. She brought along her son David, who was Clayton's age, and helped us find our seats and settle in. As soon as the previews began, I inconspicuously pulled out the earbuds attached to the Walkman hidden discreetly in my bag. I could hear Becky and the boys giggling and I knew all six eyes were focused on the screen. So I pressed play and began to listen to the tape.

The speaker's name was Marolyn Ford. She was a few years older than me, but her story was painfully familiar. She spoke of slowly losing her sight and described her emotions and challenges in a way I recognized all too well. She shared about her life as a wife and mother and about how tired she was of being blind. I knew how she felt. I, too, had slowly lost my sight. I, too, was a wife and mother. And I, too, was so, so tired. Blindness is draining. Even as I sunk into the theater seat, tiredness had washed over me. It wasn't a physical tiredness but an emotional, mental, and spiritual fatigue that was zapping me. And just keeping my sadness and frustration in check is emotionally draining all by itself. Trying to remember phone numbers, appliance buttons, my schedule, my to-do list, where I am walking, and where I place things so I can find them again are all reasons blindness is mentally draining. And then there's the spiritual fatigue. Loving God and hating blindness, and wanting to trust God while wondering why he hasn't healed me, make me live in a perpetual state of spiritual weariness.

So there I sat, identifying completely with Marolyn Ford. But there was a point in her message when every part of me wanted to turn off the tape. I knew she was about to describe the one part of her story I would *not* be able to relate to—something that would feel like salt on my open wound. But for some reason I kept listening.

In the darkness of the theater, in the darkness of my blindness, I listened to her describe the night she cried out to God for healing. She shared how she and her husband had prayed. She then described how, after praying, she could see again. She could see not just a little bit but completely.

Tears welled up in my eyes. She continued to tell the story of how she went to the eye doctor after her healing, and the doctor gasped as he confirmed that she could see—even though she had no retina. Her healing was a full-blown, certifiable, unreasonable miracle!

Tears were now streaming down my cheeks. How could I reconcile God's decision to heal the blindness of one of his children but not the other? How could I carry the joy I felt for what God *could* do in the same heart that breaks because of what God *won't* do?

I was genuinely happy for Marolyn because I knew intimately what she had received and the burden she was now free of. I really was astonished and thanked God for her healing. But I also felt a piercing sorrow. Becky, Clayton, and David had no idea what was happening next to them in the theater that day, but I have never forgotten it.

I came face-to-face with one of the hardest questions of faith: *Why one and not the other?*

Deep down, I didn't think it had anything to do with Marolyn's faith versus my faith. Nobody deserves healing based on their degree of faith or lack of faith. The faith we have is a gift of God's grace. Would God give her a bigger gift than he gave me just so she could please him more and therefore receive more from him? That didn't make sense.

My sorrow wasn't because I was jealous. Really, I wasn't. With all I knew about how hard it is to be blind, I was genuinely happy for her. But my sorrow was because we loved the same God and had the same eye condition, but we had very different outcomes. She was healed; I was still blind.

Why?

As the movie was coming to a close, I wiped away my tears and asked God for composure. I just didn't want to talk about it with anyone that day. In fact, I have never talked about it until now. It was such an intimate, raw, hard moment between me and God.

I had to confront the unfairness of the God I loved. I didn't want to feel those emotions and question my faith. I just wanted to paste a mushy greeting card over that very broken place in my heart, which read, "Let go and let God."

But I couldn't—and I didn't.

Instead, I had to face up to the question, *God, are you fair?*

CHAPTER 1

Just Desserts

Life is never fair, and perhaps it is a good thing for most of us that it is not.

Oscar Wilde, *An Ideal Husband*

As a little girl in church, I used to sing the beautiful hymn, "Fairest Lord Jesus." I loved the melody, and even though I didn't really grasp the words, I liked them too.

Fairest Lord Jesus, ruler of all nature,
O Thou of God and man the Son,
Thee will I cherish, Thee will I honor,
Thou, my soul's glory, joy, and crown.

I had no idea what "my soul's glory, joy, and crown" were, and I didn't much care. All I cared about was that Jesus was the "fairest"! And since Jesus and I were tight, I expected things should work out pretty well for me. Fairness was really important to me, as it is to most children. I didn't want my brothers to get more candy than I did or to stay up later than I got to. I just wanted everything to always be fair. So it was reassuring to think of Jesus as he was described in that hymn — the "fairest."

I clearly didn't understand that the hymn writer was using another definition of *fair* — beautiful, lovely, and pleasing. Bummer! But shouldn't Jesus still be described as the fairest anyway? After all, he is God, and God is fair, right? Yet, bad things happen to people all the time. And bad things happen to Christians too — people who are tight with God. So is God fair?

In the summer of 2010, Joni Eareckson Tada, a woman I have long admired, was diagnosed with breast cancer. More than thirty years ago, her book about the diving accident that left her a quadriplegic was one of the last books I read before I was diagnosed with the degenerative eye disease that took the majority of my vision. Her story inspired me, and reading about how she struggled, questioned, and triumphed over her limitations was exactly what I needed tucked into my heart for my coming journey into darkness. I have loved her ever since, so I was saddened when I heard about her cancer. I thought, "She doesn't deserve that pain. She's been in a wheelchair since she was seventeen. Isn't that suffering enough? She has served God so faithfully, even with her disability. It just doesn't seem fair that God would let her get cancer. Isn't one hard thing in this life enough?"

We tend to feel like a little suffering is expected, but once we've met the Christian quota for suffering, it just isn't fair to have more piled on. Besides, don't we as Christians deserve protection, blessings, and healing from "fairest Lord Jesus"? And not just us—there are plenty of people who may not be Christians, but they don't deserve a bum rap either. You know, like how a dad loses his job at the same time his elderly mom has to be put in a nursing home, while his young son struggles with a new diagnosis of diabetes and his wife is so overwhelmed that she falls into a deep depression. And of course, with no job, there is no insurance. How is *that* fair? How can "good" people deserve such bad things in life? Especially when we believe God is good?

Many of us embrace the belief that we deserve good things from God because he is good and that seems only fair. But is it really true? Yes, God *is* good, but does this mean we *deserve* only good things in our lives?

What Do We Deserve from God?

I've never grappled with this issue of what we deserve from God as much as I did when I sat in the front of the auditorium in a civic center on a cold January night. I was the guest speaker at a women's conference. I had just completed the first of three talks, and it had already been a hard weekend. The travel had been challenging; the weather was raw and wintry; and now a striking theological difference between me and the conference organizers had sparked an undercurrent of tension in the room.

The tension had to do with our differing views of healing. One group of Christians reads the Bible and is convinced it is God's will that everyone be healed. Other Christians read the same Bible and conclude it is not God's will that everyone be healed. If you're unfamiliar with the Bible, this may be confusing. Here's a very simplified synopsis of the two basic ways Christians understand sickness and healing.

- View 1: Some believe all sickness should be healed. When healing does not occur, they believe it can be attributed to either a lack of repentance for sin or a lack of faith. If you have enough faith, God will heal you. Because of your faith and God's goodness, you deserve healing.
- View 2: Others believe God allows sickness and suffering, and both can be redeemed by God for a purpose. But it is not God's will that all should be healed on planet Earth. Sickness isn't necessarily a result of individual sin or a lack of faith, but rather a result of our broken human condition. Suffering and healing are not based on merit. In general terms, we aren't sick because we deserve it, and we aren't healed because we deserve it.

I happen to fall into the View 2 camp. But the majority of the women in the auditorium on that January weekend fell into the View 1 camp. It was clear that someone on the "choose the speaker" committee had failed to inform the leadership that I might have a slightly different perspective on what the Bible says about healing. Oops! I guess I just assumed that any group that invited a blind speaker to their event would know they were getting the walking poster child for the "God doesn't always heal" perspective.

My feeling that the woman in charge didn't agree with my understanding of Scripture was confirmed as the weekend went on. Following my first talk, in which I shared my story of living with blindness and living with faith, the woman responsible for putting on the conference stood on the platform and graciously offered a subtle theological rebuttal. I felt a tad uncomfortable, but I tried to keep smiling and chalk it up to sisterly differences. *It's OK*, I thought. *She's entitled to share her opinion. It's no big deal.*

My second talk was based on the story of Shadrach, Meshach, and Abednego in Daniel 3—the story in which three Hebrew men are thrown into the fiery furnace by angry King Nebuchadnezzar and then rescued by God. My key point was that sometimes God chooses to deliver us *through* fire rather than *from* fire. When I finished my talk, any thoughts I had that our differences were no big deal had vanished. I could tell by the atmosphere in the room that it was, in fact, a very big deal. I suddenly felt like my name would soon appear on the church's "most wanted" list. This time when the woman in charge took the stage after I finished speaking, she was slightly less gracious in the way she refuted my teaching. I was clearly in trouble.

The conference leader and I couldn't have been more opposite in our understanding, and here I was saying things like, "Sometimes God does not heal," and, "Sometimes God brings you through the fire." I didn't want to cause confusion for the audience and, truthfully, I didn't want to cause trouble for myself with the woman in charge—because, believe me, she was large and in charge! I just wanted to be faithful to the truth as I understood it and then leave. I am quite sure they wanted the same. At least I'm sure about the *leave* part.

There was a thirty-minute break before the third session, and I used every minute of it to pray about my final message. It was about the apostle Paul's thorn in the flesh—you know, the thorn God didn't remove (2 Corinthians 12:7–9). *Oh no*, I thought. *The woman in charge isn't going to like this message at all! Should I soften it, Lord?* As I prayed, I felt like God was giving me a green light to give the talk as it was, so I walked to the podium for the last session and asked the women to turn to 2 Corinthians 12 in their Bibles. I have never felt so small, so aware of my own frailty, so willing to be wrong—and so willing to be *out of there*! As I began, I was still silently asking God to give me wisdom or to pluck that thorn right out of Scripture. But no matter how hard I tried to see it otherwise, the thorn remained. So I proceeded to teach about living a life of faith when God allows thorns.

By the end of the message, I felt enormously relieved. It was over—or so I thought. Turns out it was just beginning. The formerly gracious woman in charge stood and said in an unmistakably condescending tone, "I would like to thank our little speaker." *Our little speaker?* I suddenly felt like a Shrinky Dink who wanted nothing more than to become the invisible woman. But there I sat, red with embarrassment and hurt, and just a little incredulous.

Did she really just call me "our little speaker"? I'm toast! The heat was on. I braced myself for another rebuttal, but instead of refuting my message, she pulled out the big guns. "Everyone in this room deserves to be healed," she stated. "If you have enough faith, God will heal you."

My heart began to race. Actually, my heart began to break. *What about Paul?* I thought. *He had faith, but he wasn't healed. What about the Hebrew men thrown into the furnace? God allowed that. How could she disregard all the examples in the Bible?*

Then came the moment of truth—her truth anyway. After revving up everyone's emotions, the leader announced, "If you believe you deserve to be healed, stand. Come on, stand! You deserve to be healed. Stand up and show God you have the faith to be healed. You deserve it!" Women were clapping as other women in the room rose to their feet.

I felt a clammy sweat in the palms of my hands, and my heart was still pounding. *I was in the front row!* Everyone could see "our little speaker." Even if they couldn't easily see me, they would be looking for me, because the leader's invitation was in direct opposition to the message I had just invited them to consider. Women all over the auditorium were standing, weeping, and cheering. The woman in charge kept inviting them to stand, repeatedly declaring that they "deserved to be healed."

The atmosphere in the room was intense, and I was a knot of tension. I stared straight ahead and tried to whisper like a ventriloquist to my friend Karen, who was seated next to me, "Is everyone standing?" Karen whispered through her own pursed lips, "Everyone but us." She paused for a second and then whispered, "I'll do whatever you do."

How I hated to go against the group. How I hated to be obvious, looking as if "our little speaker" was trying to make a big theological statement. And how I hated to upset the woman in charge with the very big personality and the very loud microphone. I wanted Karen to say, "Aw, c'mon, let's just stand. It won't really matter. It'd be better to compromise by standing than to upset everyone by sitting." But she didn't say that, and I'm glad she didn't.

Let's just say "our little speaker" was shaking in her size six boots. I sighed and whispered back to Karen, "I can't stand." Her response was my consolation: "Neither can I." And so there we sat. Heathens or heretics—I'm not sure what the onlookers thought about us. I just know that, according to Karen, we were the only two sitting.

The reason I remained seated had nothing to do with faith. Had the invitation been "if you believe God can heal," or something similar, I would have been on my feet. Actually, I may have been standing on my chair and shouting so loudly I would have gotten on everyone's nerves. Because of God's grace, I have been granted faith. The faith I have is sufficient faith for healing—and it's sufficient faith for suffering.

My friend, the reason I didn't stand was because of the way the leader consistently made her appeal: "You deserve to be healed." I did not stand because I don't believe I deserve to be healed. Is that radical? Does it sound like low spiritual self-esteem or a martyr complex to you? As you consider this, let me reassure you that there have been many times when I have gratefully received prayers for healing. Mighty men and women of faith have laid hands on me and prayed as tears streamed down my face. I have exercised the faith to be healed, but my requests for divine healing are not motivated by the belief that I deserve it.

Think about it. If you had been at that conference, would you have stood? Do you feel you deserve to be healed—or delivered or blessed? If you do, please don't think I am condemning you or your views. After all, it may simply indicate that those who hold this view see God as loving, powerful, and good—and he is. I know the weeping women in the auditorium that wintery night weren't calculating their own merit when they stood for healing. It's likely most didn't even register the implications of the way the leader phrased her appeal. They stood because they longed to be rescued from their heartbreak. They were showing God they loved and trusted and needed him. I respect them for their faith and devotion. But standing because you *believe* God can heal you and standing because you believe you *deserve* for God to heal you are two very different things.

So here's a question: What do you and I really *deserve* from God? As you ponder that question, let me introduce you to two guys from the Old Testament whose story gives us a clue about what we deserve.

Deserve or Desserts?

Moses had an older brother named Aaron. The Lord had appointed Aaron, his four sons, and his descendants to serve as Israel's priests (Exodus 28). The primary function of priests was to oversee the offering of sacrifices to God. Because of his holiness, God had instituted strict protocols for everything to do with worship and how the priests should approach him (Leviticus 1–9). One day, Aaron's two oldest sons evidently decided to approach God on their terms: "Nadab and Abihu took their censers, put fire in them and added incense; and they offered unauthorized fire before the LORD, contrary to his command" (Leviticus 10:1).

Exactly what Aaron's sons did isn't totally clear, but this we do know — it wasn't what God required. When they offered "unauthorized fire before the LORD," Aaron's sons dishonored God by ignoring the very specific rules he had established for worship in the tabernacle. At best, their actions were careless; at worst, they showed flagrant disregard for God.

Sometimes we think of God as a doting grandpa in the sky who chuckles good-naturedly at our sinful actions because he considers them merely silly or cute. Other times we think of God as an unconcerned deity who pays attention only to the big moral violations in the world like theft and murder. And then there are times we think of God as someone who shouldn't be too picky about what we do because, after all, we mean well most of the time and we're only human. Maybe those are some of the thoughts Aaron's sons had as they brought their strange fire to God. Perhaps they didn't take him seriously, so they thought he probably wouldn't take them too seriously either. But they were dead wrong, literally: "Fire came out from the presence of the LORD and consumed them, and they died before the LORD" (Leviticus 10:2).

What? They improvised a little on the rules and God struck them dead? That's not what they deserved, is it? They didn't mean to tick off God. How could such a seemingly minor infraction warrant the death penalty? As much as it pains me to say it, Nadab and Abihu got their just desserts. They got what they deserved. They violated the law of the holiness of God, and God responded justly. They deserved to be treated according to their sin.

We, too, deserve to be treated according to our sin. Yet we don't get what we deserve. God treats us "unfairly" when it comes to our sin. We all play with unauthorized fire. We live our lives with all manner of actions and attitudes that affront God's character. Simply put, we come before God with sin.

In and of themselves, our sins may not seem like a big deal — they're just part of being human. But what they reveal is that we have a sinful nature; we have the inclination and disposition to sin. Consequently, our sinful actions and attitudes are just like that unauthorized fire Aaron's sons carted into God's presence. Neither the strange fire—nor its owner—can stand before God because both are sinful.

The psalmist put it like this: "If you, LORD, kept a record of sins, Lord, who could stand?" (Psalm 130:3). I'll answer his question: Not me. And not you either. None of us can stand before God in our sinfulness because he is holy.

And, my friend, that's why I didn't stand that night in the civic center. I am, by my very nature, a lawbreaker who deserves what Aaron's sons received. "For the wages of sin is death," is how the apostle Paul explained it to the church in Rome (Romans 6:23).

The teaching of Scripture is that we are all sinners: "All have sinned and fall short of the glory of God" (Romans 3:23). Think of it this way: If you were a garbage collector, you would collect garbage, right? Consequently, you earn a garbage collector's wage. Just like one who collects garbage is a garbage collector, one who sins (and that's all of us) is a sinner. Garbage collectors earn a wage based on who they are and what they do. Sinners also earn a wage based on who they are and what they do. The wages of our sin is death. But as sinners, you and I don't get paid according to what we do. Even though we earn death from our sin, we don't get that wage deposited in our accounts. We could call it "unfair." God says, "I will forgive their wickedness and will remember their sins no more" (Hebrews 8:12).

God forgives us our sins even though we don't deserve forgiveness. He gives us mercy instead of punishment; he offers us life rather than death. God "does not treat us as our sins deserve or repay us according to our iniquities" (Psalm 103:10). The reason we don't get treated the way our sins deserve is because Jesus was treated that way on our behalf instead. Jesus Christ received the "wage" of sin that was due to us. He took on himself what he did not deserve when he died on the cross so we wouldn't have to.

Thankfully, God is not fair.

So back to the "little speaker" incident. As I sat there while everyone around me stood, I couldn't help but think about what I deserved. I thought about the wages of my sin. I deserved death. I knew that. I couldn't stand because I knew I didn't deserve healing; I deserved something far worse. Technically, I deserved hell. But, thankfully, God is not fair. He does not give me, and he does not give you, what we deserve.

Let me make sure I am really clear here because I know this is a tough subject. You do not suffer because somewhere in the mind of God he has decided, *Oh, she is such a sinner that she deserves to suffer.* I am in no way suggesting that you *deserve* suffering. What I am attempting to do is shift your gaze to the bigger and deeper truth. We all deserve separation from God, which is the worst suffering the human soul can endure. He didn't give us that. So, if he allowed suffering in your life, even that hard place can be a place of God's mercy in your life. God may heal you if that is your struggle—and I hope he does! I know God can heal me. I want God to heal me. But if he chooses to, it won't be because I've earned it, impressed him with my big faith, or deserve it; it will be because his sovereign mercy decides it. The psalmist writes, "The Lord is compassionate and gracious, slow to anger, abounding in love" (Psalm 103:8).

My friend, I know what I've written about what we do and don't deserve may be a heavy truth to bear. But I invite you to view the weight of it as an anchor that grounds you rather than as a millstone that pulls you under. The wonder, humility, and freedom that come from embracing this truth can help you rest within your sorrow or suffering. Just because you don't deserve to be healed doesn't mean you won't be healed. In his mercy and wisdom, God will always give you his best. He made that clear once and for all on the cross of Calvary.

If you feel weighed down and burdened, look to Jesus and his cross—focus on the generous love it represents. When you're really hurting, think about what you really deserved and thank him for what you got instead. You got grace; you got peace; and you got unconditional love that will carry you through any sorrow. And both you and I got the best gift of all—fairest Lord Jesus.

CHAPTER 2

Divine Inequality

Dad: "The world isn't fair, Calvin."
Calvin: "I know, but why isn't it ever unfair in my favor?"

Bill Watterson, *Calvin and Hobbes*

I used to believe everything I read in the parenting books—and then I had kids. All the information I'd absorbed didn't make me a better parent—just a more confused and insecure one. Can I get a witness? Amen. Anyway, I have often wished the Bible had a parenting appendix with a solution for every possible situation. For example, "If thy son talketh backeth disrespectfully, giveth him four minutes in time-out for each word spoken." Or, "If thy child spitteth out her green beans at dinner, withhold the dessert Twinkies from her belly." Or, "If your son and his friends throweth green slime all over your basement at his thirteenth birthday party, thou shalt ..." I'm sure the inspired appendix would offer the perfect response for such a violation. Phil and I were on our own, though, when it came to dealing with our slime-covered basement.

The sleepover was fun for Clayton and his four friends. They watched movies, ate pizza, and went to an arcade—where one of the boys won a jar of green slime. Phil and I left them in the basement at about midnight. As we got ready for bed, we heard the typical sounds of adolescent boys from the subterranean sanctuary—laughing, shooting Nerf guns, and playing bass-pounding video games.

Saturday morning, the party continued as the boys got ready to head out for a game of basketball. That's when Phil went downstairs and discovered it hadn't been Nerf guns we'd heard the night before, but a slime war of monumental proportions. Green gunk was splotched all over our basement—the mantel, the couch, the rug, the pool table, the boys' shoes, and even the pizza boxes. Seemingly, nothing had escaped the scourge of sticky pea-green glop. When Phil questioned the boys, they confessed to the slime war. Phil had tried to wash out one of the stains, and it was obvious it would be a lengthy project.

So Phil gathered the boys and made this pronouncement: "Men, I planned to wash my van today, but now I won't have time because I'll be cleaning the slime out of the basement. So instead of playing basketball, you get to finish the party by washing our van." Resigned to their fate, Clayton's friends quietly marched outside, sponges and buckets in hand. But Clayton wasn't ready to give in. An experienced negotiator, he pulled his dad aside and argued how unfair it was to make them wash the van (which was in the driveway outside for *all* the neighbors to see) instead of just cleaning the basement (which was downstairs inside so *none* of the neighbors could see—and the "neighbors" included several cute girls Clayton's age. Get the point?). But Phil explained how much easier washing the van was for them than detoxing the basement was for Phil. Clayton and Phil had very different interpretations of what was fair.

Unfairness is often a matter of perspective, isn't it? And let's face it, most of the time it's only *our own* perspective that matters to us. When a coworker gets the raise we feel we deserve—unfair. When someone else gets credit for our good idea and we are overlooked—unfair. When men's hairlines get higher while women's bustlines get lower—unfair. You get the idea. And when that unfairness shows up in the really personal or painful areas of life, we often put the blame for it squarely on God's shoulders—and that's when the issue of fairness reaches a whole new level.

When God answers one mom's prayer and not another mom's prayer—that seems unfair. When one child dies of leukemia as another child experiences a successful bone marrow transplant—

that seems unfair. If a person who lives with integrity and kindness has terrible flood damage to their home and no insurance, while the lowlife living next door gets just a little water damage and a fat check from the insurance company—which they then blow on lottery tickets—it can seem really unfair. When your TV screen fills with pictures of precious children living in a land of famine—starving and orphaned—is that fair? When a helpless elderly person is abused by someone they trust, how can anyone think God is fair and just? When such things happen, isn't it just natural to question whether or not God is fair?

A Disturbing Parable

God knew we would grapple with thorny questions about his alleged unfairness. That's why Jesus tells a disturbing parable about a landowner and a vineyard (Matthew 20:1–16).

Early one morning, a landowner hired several day laborers to work in his vineyard. After agreeing on a denarius for a full day's labor, they all headed to the vineyard, and the workday began. Later that morning, the landowner went out again and hired more workers for his vineyard. They, too, agreed to work for a denarius. Three more times throughout the day, the landowner went out and hired even more workers.

When evening came and the work was complete, the workers lined up to be paid. Beginning with those hired last, the landowner paid each one a denarius. He progressed through the labor pool and finally reached the first laborers he'd hired at daybreak—those who had clearly worked the longest. Seeing how generous the boss had been with the late arrivals, all the sunburned men who had been there the longest, toiled the hardest, and sweated the most were anticipating that the boss would do something extra generous for them. But when he handed them their wages, each one received just one denarius—the same amount as the dudes who barely broke a sweat and went home after only an hour or two of work. *What?* There is no way that's fair! The early-bird workers certainly didn't think it was fair. Jesus said, "When they received [the denarius], they began to grumble against the landowner" (Matthew 20:11). I don't know about you, but I think I would have grumbled too.

The wage situation doesn't seem fair because all the workers were paid equally, even though they hadn't done equal amounts of work. The disgruntled workers told the landowner, " 'These who were hired last worked only one hour,' they said, 'and you have made them equal to us who have borne the burden of the work and the heat of the day' " (Matthew 20:12).

Those who had labored for a full day focused on how unfair it was to give equal pay for unequal hours. Question for you: Are being treated *equally* and being treated *fairly* the same things? Hold that thought and let's pop back to the vineyard.

The laborers accuse the landowner of unequal and unfair treatment, and the landowner's response seems as offensive as his actions: "I am not being unfair to you, friend. Didn't you agree to work for a denarius? Take your pay and go. I want to give the one who was hired last the same as I gave you" (Matthew 20:13 – 14). Wow. That just doesn't seem fair to me. How about you? Though it is just, it just doesn't seem fair. Hmmm.

Fair or Just?

This parable points a questioning finger from the vineyard straight to our own hearts: Do we disapprove of God's sense of fairness when it doesn't line up with our own? The landowner reminded his fuming workers that he did exactly what he promised he would do. These laborers got angry and felt the owner was unfair in comparison to what their fellow workers got.

We often use comparison to determine fairness, don't we? But is that really the best measure? Comparisons are typically based on personal experience, and they're always subjective. Consequently, what seems unfair to one (like the worn-out guys who worked from sunrise to sunset for a denarius) may seem perfectly right and fair to others (like those who worked an hour and also got a denarius).

Rather than playing the comparison game, perhaps the real question you and I should ask—and the question the workers should have asked—is not "Is the master *fair*?" but "Is the master *just*?" In other words, *Did the master do as he said he would?*

The workers grumbled against the landowner because receiving equal pay for unequal work left them feeling like they weren't fairly compensated. However, if the morning workers had based their assessment on the master's justice rather than on their view of fairness, they might have reached a different conclusion.

When we ask the question of fairness, it is usually a self-centered inquiry. What we're really asking are questions like, "Is this fair to me?" "Was I treated as I expected?" "Did they get more than I did?" However, when we ask the question of fairness from the perspective of justice, it is a God-centered inquiry. "Is God right in all his ways?" "Did God do as he said?" "Is God being consistent with his Word?"

The master in the story paid the workers exactly what he'd promised—he was *just*. He did not lie. It would have been grossly unjust if the owner had lied by promising one denarius and giving less than that or none at all. But he didn't lie. And God doesn't lie either (Numbers 23:19; Titus 1:2).

God is *just*, even when he doesn't seem *fair*.

Can you embrace that truth? Embracing the mystery of God's just inequality can save you from bitterness that will wither up your soul and from resentment that will keep you chained to self-centeredness. That is no way to live, I promise you.

So when you feel like God is treating you unfairly, anchor yourself in these truths:

- God's ways and works are perfect and just; he is faithful to me (see Deuteronomy 32:4).
- God's way and word are perfect and flawless; he will be my shield and refuge (see Psalm 18:30).
- God doesn't change; I won't be destroyed (see Malachi 3:6).

My friend, you can trust God's promise to you, for he will never lie. The psalmist affirms, "The LORD is righteous in all his ways and faithful in all he does" (Psalm 145:17). Trust his just character even when you don't understand your circumstances or God's purpose. The laborers in the parable may not have understood the landowner's motives, methods, or the meaning of his actions, but what matters most is that the master was faithful to his promise.

The same applies to you and me. You may not always understand God's motives, methods, or the meaning behind his actions in your life. I sure don't! But I do trust him, and so can you. He is always faithful.

Years later, our family still talks about Clayton's thirteenth-birthday disaster—uh, I mean, party. When the guys look at the photos, along with pictures of the boys shooting pool and eating pizza, they laugh at a few very funny photos of the young partiers with forlorn faces washing the family van. Though we giggle now, Phil and I still wonder if we handled it correctly. And Clayton is still not convinced we did! You know what conclusion we always come to? Phil is not a perfect father so he can and does make mistakes. But God is a perfect Father. We can trust that he will always, always, always be just—even when things don't seem fair. God is just in the way he cares for each of his children. We can rest in his just, righteous, and merciful character.

CHAPTER 3

Justice Delayed, Justice Denied

When God acts justly, he is not doing so to conform to an independent criterion, but simply acting like himself in a given situation. As gold is an element in itself and can never change nor compromise but is gold wherever it is found, so God is God, always, only, fully God and can never be other than he is.

A. W. Tozer, *Knowledge of the Holy*

A supermarket parking lot just outside of Tucson, Arizona; the Century movie theater in Aurora, Colorado; a shopping mall in Clackamas, Oregon; Sandy Hook Elementary School in Newtown, Connecticut. These are all locations of mass shootings in America. The total number of innocent people killed was forty-seven, and that is forty-seven too many.

I don't know about you, but just thinking of these horrific acts and the slaughter of innocent victims raises painfully challenging questions for me. *Does justice really prevail in this world? And if so, when does it kick in? Is God really good and in control?* When innocent people suffer, it's hard to believe that a just God could be sovereign over all the evil chaos.

So, *is* God really just?

For generations, even the heroes of our faith have asked some version of this question. King David asked God, "How long will you defend the unjust and show partiality to the wicked?" (Psalm 82:2). And even Job was quoted by his friend Elihu as saying, "I am innocent, but God denies me justice" (Job 34:5). The prophet Habakkuk said to God, "Your eyes are too pure to look on evil; you cannot tolerate wrongdoing. Why then do you tolerate the treacherous? Why are you silent while the wicked swallow up those more righteous than themselves?" (Habakkuk 1:13).

These heroes of faith asked God how long he would show partiality to the wicked and allow them not only to remain but to prevail over the righteous. They voiced the confusion we all feel when we try to reconcile belief in a just God with the injustice we experience all around us. And God knew we would wonder about such things. I believe that's part of the reason Jesus told a parable about a widow and an unjust judge. The story encourages us to keep pressing on in prayer, and it also illustrates what injustice looks and feels like (Luke 18:1–6).

The Widow and the Unjust Judge

Day in and day out, a widow came to a judge who "neither feared God nor cared what people thought," begging him, "Grant me justice against my adversary" (Luke 18:2–3). Evidently, the judge wasn't a nice guy. And he clearly wouldn't have been described as fair or just. In fact, today, even if he had somehow managed to be appointed as a judge, his failure to rule justly would quickly have led to him being disbarred. Chances are, the judge was taking bribes or perhaps even trying to curry favor with the widow's adversary. Whatever the case, Jesus' story paints the picture of a powerful and ruthless man pitted against one of the least powerful and most vulnerable members of society.

Widows in first-century Palestine were often treated unjustly. Unlike today, when a widow might have a pension, life insurance, or even a good job, widows in Jesus' day were left to the mercy of their husbands' relatives. A widow had no legal right to any of the property or possessions that had belonged to her husband. Everything automatically reverted to his closest male relative—a grown son, a father, a brother, etc. You get the idea. If the husband's family was unkind or didn't like her, a widow was in big trouble.

In Jesus' story, the judge who could intervene and grant justice refused to even hear the widow's case. He ignored her and sent her away. But she refused to give up. Day after day, she went back and banged on his door. Eventually, what she couldn't accomplish by power she accomplished by persistence. She simply wore the man down to the point that he was ready to give her whatever she wanted just so she would leave him alone. He said to himself, "Because this widow keeps bothering me, I will see that she gets justice, so that she won't eventually wear me out with her coming!" (Luke 18:5 NIV, 1984 ed.). The weak little widow conquered the big bad judge. I love that!

Now, of course, this is just a story. But Jesus' hearers back then would have immediately identified with it. They knew women like that poor widow, and they certainly knew of unjust judges. And so do we. We all know people who are treated unjustly and people who thwart or withhold justice from others. In fact, you may know exactly how that widow felt because you feel like that right now.

So what is the point of the story? I bet that's what Jesus' hearers were wondering too. I can just imagine being in the audience when Jesus got to this point. I bet they were waiting for the "gotcha!" — and Jesus didn't disappoint them. He said, "And will not God bring about justice for his chosen ones, who cry out to him day and night? Will he keep putting them off? I tell you, he will see that they get justice, and quickly" (Luke 18:7–8).

OK, let's get real here. Jesus said God will see that we get justice "quickly," right? Does it feel like God's justice has come quickly to meet you in your heartache? Do you think the widow with the red, puffy knuckles raw from knocking felt like the judge rendered justice "quickly"? My friend, I know it doesn't often *feel* like justice is quick. I get tired of being blind. I know you get tired of dealing with the stress, sadness, and frustration that come with your heartaches too. It's hard to patiently endure what God allows, but God promises he will render justice on your behalf, in his perfect way and time. Solomon once wrote, "I said to myself, 'God will bring into judgment both the righteous and the wicked, for there will be a time for every activity, a time to judge every deed'" (Ecclesiastes 3:17). The wise king affirmed that even if it feels like God isn't responding quickly, he is active and will be faithful in bringing about justice for you. My friend, sometimes God's "quickly" isn't our "quickly." I get that. But I will keep on knocking and trusting and believing. Will you?

What to Do While You Wait for "Quickly"

When faith gets hard because of unanswered questions, God's apparent lack of fairness, or even your own fatigue from carrying a burden way too long, it's hard to hang on and keep trusting God. How do you just keep knocking patiently in faith, hoping the door of justice will open for you? What do you do in the meantime? My friend Lena was in that kind of place in her marriage, and Lena made three choices that helped her. When I have been in really hard places, these are choices I have made, and I hope they can help you too.

1. Cry When You Hurt

After twenty years, Lena and Marcus's marriage had deteriorated to a cold, hard association. Neither felt safe with the other, and they both feared more heartbreak. Lena confessed that she had run out of tears. She felt hopeless. As we talked, she admitted that perhaps the reason she had no more tears was because her heart had become a walled fortress. "Nothing gets in, and nothing gets out," she said. As we walked this hard journey together, she slowly began to soften and allow her heart to feel, and when she did, she would just cry. At first her tears made her feel out of control, but really what they revealed was that she was finally beginning to trust that God was in control. She believed he would act justly in her pain and for her marriage.

Do you identify with Lena? Are you in a hard place where it just plain hurts and feels hopeless? Don't deny your hurt or try to diminish it. Honesty and vulnerability lead to intimacy, but repression leads to isolation and depression. Humbly admit your disillusionment to God and to another human being who cares about you. Tears are a natural and healthy response to pain; even Jesus wept (John 11:35). When life hurts, it's OK to acknowledge your pain and cry. Your tears are safe with God.

2. Trust God More Than Your Feelings

"The scariest part for me," said Lena, "is feeling that Marcus is against me, like he is my enemy. But I submit myself to your wisdom because I know I see the world pretty blurry right now. I can't trust I am perceiving everything objectively." That was a text I received from Lena early one morning. In the midst of her trusting, knocking, and waiting, she knew deep down she couldn't totally trust her feelings. That is a humble and wise admission. I have been mired in sorrow or conflict and had the very same experience of not being able to trust my emotions. Have you?

When we find ourselves waiting for "quickly," we can experience a lot of different emotions. Our feelings are real, but they don't always reflect absolute reality. In other words, our feelings about a situation may not always match the facts of the situation. We can misunderstand, misinterpret, and become miserable because of it!

Feelings may be unreliable at times, but they are still important to acknowledge. They hint at what is in your heart and in your head. They point to what you fear and what you desire. They often reveal beliefs you didn't even know you held. So don't totally disregard them. Learn from them. What do those feelings represent? What are they inviting you to pay attention to? For Lena, her feeling that Marcus was her enemy revealed how sensitive she is to rejection.

Marcus wanted to connect with her as much as she wanted to connect with him; he was not rejecting her. But since he struggled to communicate what he was experiencing, she interpreted his signals as rejection. The rejection that Lena felt from Marcus revealed a deeper truth—she expected rejection from her husband because she had received it from her father.

Feelings can be incredibly revealing, so don't repress them. But let them serve you rather than govern you. If you let them serve you, you employ them as an intuitive detective that can lead you to ultimate truth. Feel your emotions, but don't confuse them with facts or base your faith on them. Your feelings will change; this season of pain will change. But God never does. That's why we ultimately trust him more than our feelings (2 Corinthians 5:7).

3. Choose Loyalty over Logic

"I am home," Lena e-mailed, "and it feels like just another first day of fixing my marriage all over again. I feel so anxious. I don't want my heart crushed again. I know God is in control, and I trust him, I just had no idea it would feel this scary. I will take baby steps, though. I won't give in or give up."

It would have been easier for Lena to just give up on her marriage and her faith because neither was working out well for her. But she chose not to, even though it was a hard choice to live out. The way of faith is not always the easiest way, but it is the safest and best way. That is why we remain loyal to God.

Can you choose to loyally love God and faithfully follow him, even when the path you travel doesn't make sense to you? When sorrow invades our lives, it rarely makes sense. So don't look for solace in logic. Just settle into the mystery of God by anchoring yourself to his revealed character rather than to your limited reasoning. Rest in the fact that sometimes human logic won't be enough. What God says about himself is more dependable than what you can make sense of intellectually during a time of trial.

God has been and will continue to be faithful to you. Don't miss out on the blessing that waits just around the bend by abandoning the walk of faith. As you choose to remain faithful to him, you will see his faithfulness to you more clearly.

Will Jesus Find Faith?

At the moment, Marcus and Lena's marriage is still pretty shaky. But they are home together, eating meals as a family and committed to trusting and trying. They will keep knocking and trusting that God will open the door "quickly" as they remain faithful. I am trusting God with and for them because justice will always prevail in the high court of the Most High. He promises he will be faithful. But Jesus added one more thought as he applied the lesson of this parable. It's a question he asked of his listeners then and of us now: "When the Son of Man comes, will he find faith on the earth?" (Luke 18:8).

Now that's a question that no doubt startled his disciples. How does it strike you? Will Jesus find faith on the earth when he returns? More importantly, will he find faith in you and me? That's the bigger question. Not "Will I be treated fairly?" but "Will Jesus find faith in me?" Do I trust him to be just, even when my circumstances make no sense to me? Will I choose to be loyal to him, no matter what? Will I be humbled by whatever God has allowed, and grateful for whatever sorrow I didn't receive? There are so many questions of faith that are hard to answer, but these are questions for which you *can* have the answer. You can decide what God will find in you. Will it be resentment? An entitlement mentality? Gratitude? Or will God find you faithful?

I know you want justice. So do I. We long for life to be right and righteous. The parable of the persistent widow assures us we do not cry out in vain. God is the just judge who does right at the perfect time. He hears the cries of his children. Whether we cry out to him about the injustice we see in the world around us, or out of our desire for relief from suffering, the parable of the first-century widow encourages us to keep on pressing in, to keep praying, and to keep believing.

You petition and pray to a Supreme Judge who is not only just but also merciful. Ask him for what you need, but also trust him to give you what he deems best. He will, my friend, he will.

CHAPTER 4

Stark Raving Grateful

He is a wise man who does not grieve for the things which he has not, but rejoices for those which he has.

Epictetus, *Fragments of Epictetus*

I must get some bad news out of the way before I share any good news. Brace yourself. You do not have the right to carry a live skunk into Tennessee: "It is unlawful for any person to import, possess, or cause to be imported into this state any type of live skunk, or to sell, barter, exchange, or otherwise transfer any live skunk, except that the prohibitions of this section shall not apply to bona fide zoological parks and research institutions" (Tennessee statute §70-4-208 Unlawful importation of skunks). No matter how much you want to, you just can't. Sorry.

Also, if you happen to be one of those show-off cyclists who lifts their hands from the handlebars and waves them around at people passing by, I have bad news for you too. You do not have the right to remove your hands from your handlebars when cycling in Sun Prairie, Wisconsin: "No rider of a bicycle shall remove both hands from the handlebars or practice any trick or fancy riding in any street in the city" (municipal code §10.32.020). Sorry, it's the law. Even if you don't think it's fair, you just lost your right to hotdog on two wheels.

And that's not all. In Alabama, you do not have the right to wrestle a bear. I know, I know. Now what will you do for fun if you're in Birmingham? In 2006, Alabama issued a law to prevent bear exploitation, or, more specifically, to stop bear wrestling

(Alabama code §13A-12-5). Who knew it was that big of a problem? Personally, I'd gladly give up my right to wrestle a bear. In fact, I'm pretty sure that ordinance was created not so much to protect the giant grizzly as it was to protect the numskull would-be wrestler from his own dumb self.

It gets worse, my friend. Sorry to tell you this, but if you are in Flint, Michigan, you must pull up your pants. You do not have the right to let them sag. In 2008, Flint chief of police David Dicks made headlines across the country when he ordered his officers to apprehend persons wearing sagging pants. Tighten your belt, because some exposed undies could land you in jail. If you're an American, you may think you live in the "land of the free," but apparently you still don't have the right to flaunt your droopy drawers in public.

Did you realize you had so many limitations on your rights? Personally, I have no interest in traveling with a live skunk, cycling without holding my handlebars, wrestling a bear, or wearing sloppy slacks. But neither do I like being told I don't have the right to do something—even if it's something I don't want to do!

We want our rights, don't we? And having our rights goes hand in glove with what we think of as fairness. And boy, have I heard some Christians talk about their rights. Perhaps the thing I hear Christians say most is, "I have the right to be angry."

"When my dad died," one woman told me, "I was so mad at God. But that's OK because he can handle it."

"I was so angry at God because he didn't prevent the car wreck," another woman confessed. She went on to say how she felt she was entitled to be angry at God.

"I have every right to be mad at God," a young neighbor told me years ago, "because my sister has a man, no weight problem, and everyone likes her. And me? Fat, single, and lonely."

When hard things come into our lives, there is always the possibility that our frustration can develop into bitterness. Eventually, the frustration and bitterness mutate into anger—and that anger is directed at the only one we deem blameworthy. Since God is sovereign, isn't all suffering his responsibility? If so, then shouldn't our anger be directed at God? But do we have the *right* to be angry at God?

Hmmm … Let's think about that. Do we have that right? If we do, does exercising it bring us peace? And is exercising that right really fair to God?

Our Rights and God's Rights

Do you ever think about what *God* deserves? To get some insights into this issue, let's head back to the landowner's vineyard we visited in chapter 2 (Matthew 20:1–16).

When those poor guys hired at the beginning of the day received the same wage as those hired at the end of the day, they accused the landowner of unfairness. They didn't rejoice in his generosity to the other workers or thank the landowner for keeping his promise to pay them the amount they'd agreed to. Instead, they resented the latecomers for getting the same pay for less work—and they communicated their ill feelings to the boss in no uncertain terms.

Sister (or brother), we're not so different from those angry workers; we are all capable of resentment and grumbling. I know you never do that (nudge-nudge, wink-wink), but let's continue to consider this anyway.

The master hadn't behaved like the laborers expected him to. Instead of receiving their wages with gratitude, they judged the master's decisions and found them wanting. But the master told them, "I am not being unfair to you, friend. Didn't you agree to work for a denarius? Take your pay and go. I want to give the one who was hired last the same as I gave you. Don't I have the right to do what I want with my own money?" (Matthew 20:13–15). It was the master's prerogative to compensate the workers as he did because it was his vineyard—his money, his hires, his choice.

Now think about the landowner as an image of God. Why does God have the right to do as he pleases? Here's God's response to that question:

"For every animal of the forest is mine,
   and the cattle on a thousand hills.
I know every bird in the mountains,
   and the insects in the fields are mine.
If I were hungry I would not tell you,
   for the world is mine, and all that is in it."

Psalm 50:10–12

God is the owner of all; he is the one who faithfully governs all. So, if it is his, then he has a right to do with it as he will. The prophet Isaiah reminds us that God is sovereign, and when he acts, no one prevents it (43:11–13). He has the supreme right to do as he pleases.

The landowner phrases one of the last things he says to the workers as a question: "Are you envious because I am generous?" (Matthew 20:15). Ouch! That's a potent punch line for the end of the story because it's a question that reveals the truth about the laborers' hearts.

Sometimes when we indulge what we call our right to be angry at God, what we're really doing is casting a thin veil over envy instead. Deep down, we are jealous that God is seemingly generous to someone else but not to us. We resent him for what we don't have, and rather than name our response for the dark thing it is, we justify it as righteous anger in response to God's alleged mistreatment.

It is as if we are saying that God does not have the right to do as he pleases, yet we do have the right to be mad at him when he does. What is it in your own life that you feel you have the right to be angry with God about? What if God were to ask you right now, *Don't I have the right to … let your loved one be sick? Afflict you with fibromyalgia? Make your eyes blind? Let your pain continue? Prevent your house from selling? Are you envious because I am allowing your neighbor to get a better job than yours? Healing your friend's child? Healing her eyes, but not yours?*

Wow. That's some hard stuff to swallow, isn't it? I know just reading those questions can be really difficult when your heart is broken or tender from pain and questions. I'm sorry. But, dear one, if God is the supreme Master of the universe—every star, planet, and person—he has the right to do or allow whatever he pleases.

What is God asking you through this story? I hear God asking me, *Jennifer, isn't it my prerogative and right as your Father and the King of the universe to do as I please with you? Are you judging me when my ways disappoint you because you are jealous of others or resentful of what I gave you?*

When I imagine God asking me these questions, I don't want to grumble back a response like, "I have every right to be mad at you because you haven't performed to my expectations," or "Your ways aren't good enough for me." Or, "Who do you think you are being a God I don't understand?" Instead, I want to just tell him, "I don't understand you, but I trust you and I thank you." I want to give him what he deserves. "Let them praise the LORD for his great love and for the wonderful things he has done for them" (Psalm 107:31 NLT).

God does deserve my grateful praise. He has the right to expect my gratitude. He has been good to me even in the "bad" things like blindness. He has done wondrous works—many of which I experience every day and probably even more that I am not even aware of. He sometimes allows something bad in our lives to prevent something far worse in our lives. That is a wondrous work of God I cannot even see, because sometimes I have no idea how God is working on my behalf.

Now, lest you think I am suggesting you unthinkingly say, "OK, God, got it; I won't grumble or feel any disappointment. I will just say thanks!" and just slap a happy Christian bumper sticker on your pain, let me emphasize this: Being willing to thank God doesn't mean you ignore what bothers you. It just means you are willing to look beyond what bothers you and see the good in a situation also. For example, what if those grumbly early morning workers in the parable were named Gabe and Yoshi. What if Gabe had said to Yoshi, "Man, this isn't what I expected! How about you, Yoshi?"

"Nope, Gabe, this isn't what I expected either, and I don't much like it, but at least we had work today."

"Yeah," Gabe responds, "I am thankful we got a denarius and these very attractive farmer's tans."

"Yep," Yoshi says with a nod. "The ladies love farmer's tans! I am one really thankful dude! Group hug!"

They both throw their sweaty arms around the master, thanking him for a bit of income, a promise kept, and a good day's work.

If that imaginary scenario were the case, they would not have grumbled and been resentful. Instead, they would have been grateful and given proper praise to the master who hired them and kept his promise to them.

My friend, we don't base our gratitude or praise exclusively on what we receive or do not receive from God. God deserves our praise and gratitude because of who God is. "Give thanks to the LORD, for he is good; his love endures forever" (Psalm 107:1). I give him my thanks and his due praise because he is good. His character deserves my humble gratitude.

Can you do the same?

When you look at others' lives and see that they deal with less stress, pain, or difficulty, do you resent God for being generous to them? Are you envious of their seemingly easy lives? Or can you still give him praise and thanks? Can you thank him for his wisdom and his kindness, even if it shows up more in others' lives than your own? Can you thank him for being "just," not fair? Consider this prayerfully. God understands your frailty and wants you to be free from resentment. Why? Because it hurts you. Rather than choosing resentment toward God or others, might you choose gratitude? You may have the right to be angry, but is it a right worth exercising?

Take a moment to reflect on these questions and consider how holding on to your right to be angry could be impacting you:

1. Does my anger really serve me well?
2. Does my resentment change my situation for the better?

3. Does my bitterness enhance my relationship with God and others?

4. Whom does my anger really hurt? Me? God? Others?

You and I may have the right to be angry or resentful, but sometimes fully exercising our rights isn't all it's cracked up to be. After all, you have the right to sit on a roaring campfire, but that doesn't mean you should exercise it! Choosing to forgo exercising that right and instead showing reverence to the fire will bring far more comfort and peace.

The Power of Reverence and Gratitude

We may have the right to be angry, but I would rather focus on our responsibility to be reverent. God is kind and just and deserves our respect, not our resentment. When we give him the honor he deserves by expressing our gratitude, we are the ones who receive peace and life. Now, I know it's hard to always thank God for what he does, because, quite truthfully, what he does or allows doesn't always feel so good, does it? But the good news is that you don't have to thank God *for* it if you aren't there yet. All you have to do is thank God *in* it.

In his letter to the church at Thessalonica, the apostle Paul wrote that we are to "give thanks in all circumstances" (1 Thessalonians 5:18). Choosing to be grateful is a powerful antidote to the strong and destructive influence of resentment. Think about what you have struggled with—something you felt was unfair or something you've been angry about. Could you ask God for the grace to be thankful in that situation? Paul positioned gratitude as a choice, not a feeling. My friend, even when we don't *feel* grateful, we can still *be* grateful. Through God's grace, we, too, can be thankful in all circumstances.

Being grateful *in* all things means we sincerely give thanks to God within the hard stuff. It means we have a spirit of humble thankfulness rather than seething resentment. It is really hard to resent something you are thankful for. It is almost impossible to hold a grudge or resent someone to whom you express gratitude, isn't it?

In the imaginary scenario with our new friends Gabe and Yoshi, those guys actually showed what it means to be grateful in all things. They were grateful for the wage, grateful for the work, and even grateful for the farmer's tans! The way they managed gratitude over grumbling was by focusing on the good *in* the situation and the good *in* the master. When we focus on the good *in* a situation, we, too, can be thankful. When we focus on the good *in* our Master, we, too, can be grateful and show him reverence.

May I be gut-honest with you? Choosing reverence over resentment is the only wise choice. I've been asked so many times if I resent God or am angry at God. Because I am blind, people often assume I am or have been angry with God for allowing my blindness and not yet healing it. I understand that. And, honestly, I have really thought hard about that. In fact, having been asked about it so many times, I think maybe I should be angry. But the truth is, I can't remember ever feeling angry toward God. Believe me, I have tried. I was a psychology major, for heaven's sake! I am forever searching for some dark mystery or malady within me. After studying this kind of stuff, am I not supposed to struggle with anger due to my inability to reconcile my situation? Well, I have plumbed the depths of my heart to determine why I haven't felt angry with God. Am I in denial? Have I suppressed, regressed, transferred, repressed, or digressed? No, truthfully, I haven't.

But I have found the reason. I am not angry with God because I need him too much. Call it self-preservation or call it faith; I am not sure if it isn't a bit of both. I don't resent him; I love him, and I really need him. He is my only source for true peace and hope. I would injure myself by choosing to blame him or to hold a grudge against him that created separation between us. I can be blind with God, but there is no way I can be blind without him. And when my posture is trust toward him rather than anger, I find him trustworthy and good. When I find him good, my natural response is to thank him rather than resent him.

Gratitude can break any chains of resentment that may be binding you to sorrow or bitterness. Your difficulty can be hard enough, but the resentment or anger you drag along with it can be even more debilitating than the difficulty itself. So you may have the right to be angry, but God has the right to be praised. Which choice will bring you greater peace?

My friend, gratitude to God for whatever he allows honors him. And whatever honors him blesses you. So go for it. Even through your tears, get stark raving grateful!

Threads of Truth for Your Blanket of Faith

- The LORD is righteous in all his ways and faithful in all he does. (Psalm 145:17)
- The LORD is compassionate and gracious, slow to anger, abounding in love. (Psalm 103:8)
- The LORD within her is righteous; he does no wrong. Morning by morning he dispenses his justice, and every new day he does not fail. (Zephaniah 3:5)
- For the LORD loves justice, and he will never abandon the godly. He will keep them safe forever. (Psalm 37:28 NLT)
- For the LORD will vindicate his people and have compassion on his servants. (Psalm 135:14)

Visit jenniferrothschild.com/threads to download free Scripture cards.

PART 2

God, Do You Err?

Scene 1

"You're too hard on yourself."

Those were the words my friend Joan said to me as I leaned back in the wicker chair on her back porch crying. The statement hit me in a deep place. My reaction? I was ready to beat myself up for being hard on myself! Maybe I am too hard on myself? How come?

Scene 2

Phil and I sat out on our driveway in lawn chairs. He was frustrated. I was frustrated. We have been married twenty-four years and were having a squabble. I get tired of the squabbles, and so does Phil. Our squabble escalated into a real argument. We were both heated and hurt. I don't remember what it was about now, but I do remember what Phil said to me because he had never said it before. It felt like he had put together all twenty-four years of married angst into one concentrated statement: "You're too hard on me."

Was I? "He has been hard on me too," I thought. But his comment reverberated in my mind for weeks. Am I really too hard on him? If I am, how come?

Scene 3

The doctor prescribed Wellbutrin. Full-blown depression was her diagnosis. I couldn't believe I was depressed. Me—the one who touted, "It is well with my soul," now had to modify that to, "It is Wellbutrin with my soul." Somehow, I had reached the bottom of myself and a prescription antidepressant felt like an epic fail. I felt ashamed, embarrassed, and useless.

After a few days of taking the medication and still feeling awful, I began to examine what this awful feeling might be called. I realized that what I was really feeling was guilt.

I felt guilty for needing meds.

I felt guilty for bailing on my book contract.

I felt guilty for not telling the women I speak to that I am depressed and on medication.

I felt guilty for not knowing when I would be better—or if I would ever be better.

I felt guilty for being depressed in the first place.

I felt guilty that I couldn't fix it, pray it away, or even explain it.

I felt guilty for being a burden to Phil, to my kids, to anyone who was in my world.

I listed everything I felt guilty about, and then the most painful statement I think I have ever uttered escaped my lips.

I feel guilty for being blind.

I stopped and said it again, this time as a question. *I feel guilty for being blind?* That seemed so illogical, but it was a pure, unfiltered, true feeling. I don't think depression caused it; I think depression allowed it to escape because I no longer had the energy to keep it hidden. I was stunned. How could I feel guilty for something over which I had no control? It was a painful admission. Maybe I *am* too hard on myself.

Scene 4
I am too hard on myself.

I've pondered that statement for days. I keep taking it to Jesus and asking him why I feel that way. I keep asking him to remove that lie from my thinking. When I examine that statement, I see little ways it has shown up as a core belief for many years in how I react, think, and behave.

I am hard on myself because I feel guilty I am blind. I work harder, try to compensate, shame myself when I run into a wall, scold myself if I can't remember where I put something. I am hard on myself for being blind. And I am hard on Phil because I am hard on myself.

Maybe I shouldn't be surprised by this feeling, though. I re-member when I was a teen and went to a blind psychologist. All I could think when I met with her was, "Don't create hardship for her. Don't complain." She was totally blind, and I was only legally blind. I felt guilty being in her office and having needs that were less severe than hers. How could I complain? Was that the beginning of my guilty feelings? Was that when grace exited stage left? Blind-ness gives no grace.

When I look back on these scenes, I think maybe deep down I have been hard on myself because I didn't want to be hard on God. If anyone should feel guilty because I'm blind, it's God. After all, he allowed it, and he hasn't taken it away. But his ways are perfect, right? He doesn't make mistakes, so why should he feel guilty?

Still, it's hard not to wonder, "God, do you err?"

CHAPTER 5

Wrestling with God's Ways

God's ways are higher than our ways not because he is less compassionate than we are but because he is more compassionate than we are.

Rachel Held Evans, *Evolving in Monkey Town*

I didn't expect it to affect me like it did, but it did—and it still does. It was the barely audible voice of a man I did not know that captured me. His name was Duane Miller. A friend gave me his audio recording and told me I would be amazed and encouraged. So Phil and I sat on our worn carpet, leaned back against the couch, and pressed the play button on the stereo.

Duane spoke just above a whisper as he led a Bible study on Psalm 103:

> God heals in his sovereign will. I don't know why God does the things he does. But I know that he does. And the only thing he requires from me is to allow him to be God and me to be me. And let it be. To say that every single person will always be healed because Jesus died on the cross is a misinterpretation of Scripture. On the other hand, to say that we don't have anything after the book of Acts—that miracles ended in the book of Acts and never happen again—is equally wrong. It's wrong because you have put God in a box. He doesn't want to be in a box. So the psalmist says, "I'm excited. Bless the Lord, O my soul. One of his benefits is he heals all my diseases."

At this point, Duane's voice was so strained we could hardly hear him pronounce the last few words. Then, something began to happen. As he continued to read from Psalm 103, some of the raspiness left his voice: "Praise the LORD, my soul, ... who redeems your life from the pit" (Psalm 103:2, 4). "Now, I like that verse just a whole lot," he said. "I have had, and you have had, in times past, pit experiences." And with every word, his voice became stronger and clearer. And with each enunciation, the recognition of what was happening became increasingly evident, and Duane became emotional.

"We've both had ... we've all had times when ... our lives seemed to be in a pit, in a grave ... and we didn't have ... an answer ... for ... the pit we find ourselves in." His voice was strong as he spoke. He paused frequently between words trying to gain his composure. His voice was incredibly strong, but he could barely speak because he was weeping. And on the audio, we could hear many people in the audience also beginning to cry. And so did Phil and I. We wiped our tears as Duane continued to read the psalm and then paused to say in a strong, certain voice, "I don't understand what's happening right now; I am overwhelmed at the moment. Thank you, Lord."

You see, three years previously, Duane contracted a devastating virus that infected his vocal cords. The doctors were amazed he had the ability to conjure even a whisper after the damage the virus had caused. The prognosis was that he should have been completely mute. He had endured three years with only the barest scratch of a voice and tried to adjust and keep teaching Scripture as best he could. Then God unexpectedly healed him. Word by word, a certifiable miracle of healing was captured live for all to hear. News of his healing spread quickly. Even Oprah Winfrey played the recording on her show. It was amazing! But honestly, it wasn't as encouraging as my friend had suggested it would be. I wanted it to be—I really did. I was encouraged for Duane, but hearing that miracle take place left me feeling even more disappointed.

When Phil turned off the recording, we sat in silence. After a few moments, he asked, "What are you feeling?"

Instead of saying, "I'm amazed but disappointed, happy for him but confused, and just a bit jealous," I asked the same question of Phil: "What are you feeling?"

"If God can heal him, God can heal you," he said.

"I know," I answered. But deep down, that was the problem, not the solution. I had cried tears of hope and wonder as I listened to that dear man regain his voice because I knew God could do that. But I also cried tears of loss and disappointment because I knew God had not done that for me.

Phil took my hand and said, "We should just ask God to heal you too." And we did. We both voiced our prayer for God to heal my eyes, and when Phil said the final amen, I didn't open my eyes. I waited because I dreaded opening them just in case God had not healed me. When I finally did, it was the same old darkness. Phil and I just sat a while longer in silence. It was an incredibly impactful moment for me. I can still remember how Phil and I sat on the floor, how we leaned into one another when we prayed. How I fingered the fibers of the carpet as we sat in silence after we prayed, neither of us knowing really what to say. In our stillness and silence, there was a wrestling match going on in our hearts. I was wrestling with my feelings about what God did for Duane, and with my own disappointment. I wanted to pin down my emotions and thoughts and make them fit within a Sunday school answer, but they just didn't.

Hearing such a wonderful miracle take place was a poignant reminder that God's ways are perfect yet also mysterious and not our ways. But it was also a painful reminder that sometimes his ways work out really well for someone else but not so well for us. I wanted what Duane had, but instead I got what God gave me. It reminded me of how I felt that July day in a Tallahassee theater all those years ago when I wrestled with God as I listened to another recording about a miraculous healing. Facing the hard reality that he had healed Marolyn Ford's eyes and not mine exposed such tender wounds and conflicting feelings toward God. It was so hard to admit I loved God but was disappointed in his ways. I resisted feeling the depths of my disillusionment about how God could heal Marolyn *and* me but healed Marolyn and *not* me. Obviously, this was and still is a hard question for me to resolve. With both Marolyn and Duane, I had to face what I feared, and struggle with how God's ways are perfect—but not so perfect for me.

Perhaps you, too, have wrestled with God and his ways. His ways are supposedly perfect, yet they often feel anything but perfect. So we wrestle with the *why* and *how* of his decisions—and sometimes, just like Jacob from the Old Testament, we even wrestle with God himself.

Wrestling with God

Jacob was one of the rock stars of the Old Testament. He was the son of Isaac and the grandson of Abraham. But even with such an impressive heritage, Jacob hadn't always made the best choices. In fact, his name means "usurper" or "supplanter," and he had a well-earned reputation as a trickster. Taking the advice of his manipulative mother, he deceived Isaac, his blind father, into giving the birthright inheritance to him instead of to his older twin brother Esau. That's a lot of drama and dysfunction for one family, but there's more.

Esau had vowed to kill Jacob for his treachery. Jacob then fled to Harran and stayed for many years with his uncle Laban. While there, Jacob married, had children, and got rich! Eventually, he grew homesick for his father's land, which meant he would soon come face-to-face with his very strong, very angry older brother. Although he had received God's blessing to return to his homeland, Jacob, being no dummy, sent messengers ahead to see if Esau was still intent on murder.

When the messengers returned to Jacob, they said, "We went to your brother Esau, and now he is coming to meet you, and four hundred men are with him" (Genesis 32:6).

That was definitely not the report Jacob was hoping to hear. Now it appeared that not only he but everyone he loved were as good as dead. After dividing his people and flocks into two groups, pleading with God to save them all and sending lavish gifts ahead in hopes of somehow appeasing Esau, Jacob intended to spend the night alone. Instead, he spent it wrestling.

> *So Jacob was left alone, and a man wrestled with him till daybreak. When the man saw that he could not overpower him, he touched the socket of Jacob's hip so that his hip was wrenched as he wrestled with the man. Then the man said, "Let me go, for it is daybreak."*
>
> *But Jacob replied, "I will not let you go unless you bless me."*
>
> *The man asked him, "What is your name?"*
>
> *"Jacob," he answered.*
>
> *Then the man said, "Your name will no longer be Jacob, but Israel, because you have struggled with God and with humans and have overcome."*
>
> *Jacob said, "Please tell me your name."*
>
> *But he replied, "Why do you ask my name?" Then he blessed him there.*
>
> *So Jacob called the place Peniel, saying, "It is because I saw God face to face, and yet my life was spared."*
>
> *The sun rose above him as he passed Peniel, and he was limping because of his hip.*
>
> Genesis 32:24–31

Perhaps at first Jacob might have wondered if he was being attacked by one of Esau's four hundred men. Even so, he didn't shrink back from this aggressor. His response to the attack was probably fright, but instead of choosing flight, Jacob decided to fight! A wrestling match of divine proportions ensued. And Jacob soon discovered it wasn't an enemy with whom he wrestled; it was his closest ally—"the angel" of the Lord (Hosea 12:4).

Many Bible scholars believe the angel of the Lord was a theophany or a Christophany—an appearance of the preincarnate Christ. Jesus himself was the one who wrestled with Jacob. God didn't let go of Jacob, and Jacob didn't let go of God. Jacob clung to the Lord with his whole heart and all his strength. Then God injured him so he could bless him.

Like Jacob, I have also clung to God in the darkness of my blindness and in the darkness of my confusion and disappointment.

God has injured me to bless me, and now that very injury is part of the blessing. In our living room listening to Duane's miracle and in that theater so many years ago, God was working in my heart. I knew it wasn't jealousy or depression I was wrestling with. I was not wrestling with an enemy but rather with my greatest ally. I was wrestling with God alone—the one who had allowed me to remain blind. It was God I clung to in the dark of that theater and in the silence that followed Duane Miller's miracle. And it was God who used those inner struggles to soften me, break my heart, and teach me to trust him more. He still uses the wrestling in my spirit to help me decide daily to cling to him. He uses the weariness of blindness to help me face my fears. He has taught me as I wrestle with him not to choose flight but to choose a holy fight—an unwillingness to let go of God until he uses this injury to bless me.

Can you relate to Jacob like I do? Have your wrestling matches with God and his ways left you injured? Or maybe, like me, you have struggled to make God's ways make sense? I hope like Jacob, you are choosing not to run from the potential blessing God will give you through this painful wrestling. My friend, will you fight? Will you cling to God, hold on with all your strength, and expect that whatever injury God allows will result in blessing? Can you consider your injury a source of blessing, and trust that the reason God has allowed you to struggle is so that he can bless you? Could your injury be God's perfect way of blessing you—his perfectly strange way?

The Blessing of Wrestling

It is not wrong to wrestle with God. If God allows you to wrestle with him, it is not so there will be a winner and a loser. He doesn't need to prove he is stronger and you are weaker. No. The point of wrestling with God is to give you an opportunity to cling to him. God wants you to hang on to him no matter what—and the result will be blessing. You are blessed when you bring your hurts and questions to God and struggle with them in his presence. In that divine wrestling match, you may feel wounded, but you will also receive a blessing you couldn't have received any other way.

Not every match I've wrestled ended with a quick and obvious blessing. Honestly, after praying with Phil for healing as I raked stiff carpet fibers between my fingers, I didn't jump up and scream, "Wow! What a blessing—God didn't answer my prayer! He healed Duane but not me. I am über-blessed! Whoohoo!" Not so much. But the blessing of that wrestling match came more slowly and is still with me. The blessing of peace was a result of the struggle. I have received peace from God because God used Duane's healing to give me another opportunity to make peace with him. The constant injury of blindness is that it daily presents me with the choice to make peace with God and with the fact that his ways are different from my ways. And the result of making peace with God is receiving peace from God. That is a blessing beyond measure.

So many years ago in a Tallahassee theater, I experienced an immediate blessing from my encounter with God. I left that experience feeling liberated. I was liberated from the *Why her?* and *Why not me?* questions. I was liberated from the need to deeply understand. I was freed to cling to and love a God whose ways I just didn't—and never will—understand completely.

Though I couldn't fully make sense of my experiences that day in the theater or that evening on my living room floor, I can look back now and see that God gave me the merciful opportunity to feel my pain. In private, I faced something I dreaded, which was the severe mercy and mysteries of God. And I left the encounters feeling like a wounded place in my relationship with God was beginning to heal. So perhaps I was blessed in a deeper way than Jacob was. He left the encounter with God injured but blessed. I came to God in both those instances already injured and left even more blessed. I was blessed enough to be given an opportunity to look straight into the face of blindness and straight into the face of healing and to see God in both.

Wrestling requires clinging and a determination to never let go. That is my encouragement to you, my friend. Even if you are angry, upset, afraid, or confused, cling to God. Insist on a face-to-face encounter with him. Face what you fear. Be willing to grapple with what you don't understand, and expect a blessing to follow. Don't let go until he blesses you—because he will. The only reason God wrestles with his children is to bless them.

CHAPTER 6

Perfectly Strange

We would like to take the hammer of doctrine
and take the nails of piety
and nail your feet to the floor
and have you stay in one place.
And then we find you moving,
always surprising us,
always coming at us from new directions.

Walter Brueggemann, "Not the God We Would Have Chosen"

This prayer by Walter Brueggemann beautifully expresses how God's ways aren't always what we want. Often our perception of his character confuses us. When God doesn't behave like we expect or prefer, we may think his ways are flawed. And let's be honest, there is a lot about life that really is flawed. When a teenage girl goes blind, when a baby is born with autism, when a car accident leaves a young woman a widow and a single mom, just to name a few. Are we supposed to believe that things like these are part of God's perfection? If God is perfect in all his ways, what kind of strange perfection allows such heartbreaking darkness and suffering?

Perfect?

Although the world we live in is flawed, Scripture never wavers in affirming that God does not err: "He is the Rock, his works are perfect, and all his ways are just. A faithful God who does no wrong, upright and just is he" (Deuteronomy 32:4). And then there is what God says about himself: "I form the light and create darkness, I bring prosperity and create disaster; I, the LORD, do all these things" (Isaiah 45:7). God also plainly admits his responsibility, even for things like blindness: "Who gave human beings their mouths? Who makes them deaf or mute? Who gives them sight or makes them blind? Is it not I, the LORD?" (Exodus 4:11).

So how do we explain these statements? How can he say he is responsible for things like deafness and blindness, yet also claim that he does no wrong and that his ways are perfect? How do we reconcile a perfect God with such seemingly imperfect outcomes?

Sovereignty.

That is the only answer I can find to settle my heart and help me rest in the mystery.

Surrendering to Sovereignty

When we say God is sovereign, we mean that God has all power and ultimate authority over heaven and earth. To call God sovereign is to acknowledge that no one is wiser and that no one can thwart his purpose or resist his will. Through the prophet Isaiah, God affirms his sovereignty when he says, "I make known the end from the beginning, from ancient times, what is still to come. I say, 'My purpose will stand, and I will do all that I please'" (Isaiah 46:10). And the psalmist puts it even more concisely: "Our God is in heaven; he does whatever pleases him" (Psalm 115:3).

Nothing comes into your life, into my life, or into this world without God's permission. Again, the Scriptures affirm the paradox of sovereignty: "Who has spoken and it came to pass, unless the Lord has commanded it? Is it not from the mouth of the Most High that good and bad come?" (Lamentations 3:37–38 ESV).

Whoa! If God is sovereign, does that mean that even evil comes from him?

The best example I know to address that troubling question is the biblical story of Job. Job had a surprisingly clear assessment of God and his sovereignty. I say surprisingly because he also had more than his share of loss and sorrow. And the reason he endured all that suffering was because of God's sovereignty. The story begins when Satan approaches God and challenges him about Job's faithfulness: "But now stretch out your hand and strike everything he has, and he will surely curse you to your face" (Job 1:11). It's at this point that most of us would like to hear God say something like, "No way! I will not let any harm come to Job." But instead, here is what he actually says to Satan: "Very well, then, everything he has is in your power, but on the man himself do not lay a finger" (Job 1:12). Satan, the source of all evil, had to ask permission to mess with Job. God granted it, but God also gave Satan boundaries.

Whatever heartache you wrestle with is only in your life because a sovereign God has allowed it. Satan has no ability to mess with you except as it has to do with the reins placed on him by God. It's important to make this distinction to avoid getting too caught up in what I call the "whom" of suffering. The *whom* of suffering asks, "Did God allow this, or is this from Satan?" But this is a question to which we already have an answer. We know from Scripture that "God is light; in him there is no darkness at all" (1 John 1:5). We also know that Satan is the "prince of the power of the air" (Ephesians 2:2 ESV), the ruler of "this dark world" and of "the spiritual forces of evil" (Ephesians 6:12). Evil does not originate from God because God is good (Mark 10:18). But God allows Satan to do his evil for purposes not always clear to us. When we are enduring hardship, perhaps the better questions to focus on are not about the *whom* of suffering but about the *how*:

- How will God use this redemptively in my life?
- How will he use this loss for my gain?
- How can I cooperate with my loving God's master plan through this current suffering?
- How can this possibly help me grow or change?

The *why* of suffering is sometimes never answered. But to ask the *how* of suffering allows us to begin to see the beautiful redemption of what God can do in and through our suffering.

Now, as true as that is from a biblical perspective, it may not make you feel any better. You may think, "Well, how I respond or where the trial originates is not the big deal. The big deal is the fact that God has the ability to tell Satan no but doesn't." I understand. But I also take comfort in James's assessment of God's actions toward Job: "You have heard of the steadfastness of Job, and you have seen the purpose of the Lord, how the Lord is compassionate and merciful" (James 5:11 ESV).

Think about it. Job must have really experienced God's mercy and compassion because he didn't curse God, as Satan predicted, nor did he become bitter. Job could have said, "You know, if these are God's ways, then God must not be perfect because his ways are not perfect for me. I have lost everything. I am covered with sores. My wife has abandoned me, and all I have are these self-righteous, overly talkative friends!" He could have said, "Sure, God is sovereign and allowed all this, but he isn't the kind of God I really want."

But Job didn't say any of those things. If you read the whole book of Job, you'll see that he didn't come to quick or easy conclusions. He struggled with hard emotions and confusing thoughts. But he did surrender to sovereignty. He said, "The LORD gave and the LORD has taken away; may the name of the LORD be praised" (Job 1:21). In other words, "This is God's thing! He does what he does, and I'm going to praise him anyway."

Are you willing to do that? Will you surrender to God's sovereignty? Oh, I know it isn't easy. I have asked God to help me live a life surrendered to his sovereignty. I want my hands to be open, reflecting trust and surrender rather than letting them ball into angry fists. When my hands are open to God, it's an expression that I am willing to receive what God wants to give me. And my open hands are also positioned to give him praise. Surrendering to sovereignty may not be easy, but it is best.

Think about it. Whether or not you surrender to sovereignty does not change the fact that God *is* sovereign—he is, whether or not we concede to it! So why fight it? Why not release God from our inaccurate and shortsighted assumptions and unrealistic expectations? We will experience greater peace when we love and trust a God we may not understand rather than when we constantly try to conform him into an image we have created in our imagination.

The God of My Imagination

Sometimes we think a sovereign God cannot be perfect in all his ways because his ways are not the ways of the God we wish he was. If we were to create what we might think of as our "ideal" God, we might want to create a God who is perfect according to our standards. At least, I think mine would be. My ideal God would do whatever I want and never disagree with me. At the same time, he would be smarter than me and always give me great advice. When it comes to my sins and selfishness, he would either overlook them or choose to find them quaint and amusing. He might even negotiate the standards with me. The God of my creation would stick with me no matter what and would do everything in his power to protect me and keep my life peaceful. Oh, and he would obliterate all the calories from dark chocolate and cause me to lose five pounds every time I eat a red velvet cupcake with butter cream icing! Is that really too much to ask?

And is there anything really wrong with a God like that? Think about it, the God of my creation would be a good God. He would not let people go blind. He wouldn't allow husbands and wives to ever leave their spouses for someone else. He wouldn't allow homelessness, tornadoes, or cancer. If Satan approached my kind of God with a request to mess with me, my kind of God would say, "Nope, not today—not ever!" The God I would create would be a lot more like the Candy Man. You know, "he mixes it with love and makes the world taste good." Good, right?

Or maybe that's not so good. The reason it's not so good is when you boil it all down, I really don't want a Candy Man God; I want a God like *me*! But my mini-me imaginary God would not be good for us, even if he made life only good, easy, and fun. A God made in my image would be way too much like me, and that is not the kind of

God we need. Actually, it would be really scary if God were like us. We would be subject to a fickle, flawed, and dysfunctional deity. That's not only not desirable; it's downright scary!

Creating a God according to our own standards is a dangerous thing none of us would actually seek to do. Yet sometimes the reason we are confused or frustrated with God's ways is because we unknowingly subscribe to a false notion of who he is, and deep down we think he really should be like the God we'd create if we could. After all, that would be perfect, wouldn't it?

Not.

I think we are much safer with the God of the Bible rather than the God of our imagination. God's ways can be strange, but they are strangely perfect. Because he is beyond error—God is good and perfect.

My friend, perhaps we need to have an imaginary funeral for our imaginary God. Bury him and throw away the shovel so we never dig him up again. In his place, we must lift up the Lord God Almighty. God is good and perfect. He is just and kind. It is essential that we think rightly about God and his character. God takes seriously how we perceive him, and consequently so should we. He made that pretty clear to Job's friends.

When Job was in trouble—sick, poor, depressed, lonely—his friends tried to cheer him. But their cheering turned to unsolicited advice and then to criticism. They became self-appointed experts on God's character. God didn't look kindly on these guys' interpretation of his character, though. So at the end of the book of Job, the Lord speaks plainly to one of Job's friends named Eliphaz the Temanite: "I am angry with you and your two friends, because you have not spoken the truth about me, as my servant Job has" (Job 42:7).

God takes seriously how we perceive and proclaim his character. Do you? God's ways may seem strange to us, but his ways do not have to live up to our standards or our analysis. He is who he is, and we are who we are. He is beyond error, perfect in all his ways. If his ways confuse or disappoint you, guard against the temptation to re-create him into a god you like better. You and I are to humble ourselves before him and seek to conform to his standard, not the other way around. He is sovereign and good, compassionate and merciful. If we do not accept God in his wholeness, we will never experience our own.

CHAPTER 7

Can the Immutable Change?

Thou changest not, Thy compassions they fail not:
As Thou hast been Thou forever wilt be.

Thomas O. Chisholm, "Great Is Thy Faithfulness"

When she was in high school, my friend Tammy somehow got the nickname Tammer, and it stuck. I point this out so you won't think her name is a typo. Her name really is Tammer, as in "rhymes with hammer." She has changed it for good. Her husband, on the other hand, is one of the most unchanging people I know. For example, Don has had the same job at the same company doing the same thing for twenty-four years. He's driven the same truck for a decade. In fact, when he wrecked his previous truck, he replaced it with the exact same truck—the same color and even the same year. He has eaten plain noodles since childhood—no sauces ever. He eats salads with no dressing—he never has, and I'm sure he never will!

Don actually wears the same style and brand of clothes he's worn since his twenties—and he's now pushing fifty. The same styles, the same colors—if one garment gets a hole in it, he replaces it with the exact same one. That's not too hard when all he wears are jeans and golf shirts. Thank goodness he's not still in bell-bottoms. But if the denim company deviates from their normal manufacturing process, woe be unto them, for then Don is no longer a customer. The painstaking process of potentially having to find new jeans he can wear for thirty years makes his blood pressure soar.

He has never used any tool but Craftsman from Sears. He says they are durable, and if they break, he gets a new one—the exact one. He loves the old-time Christian singers like George Beverly Shea. It's not that the new ones aren't good; it's just that he is happy with the ones he's listened to since 1972. Why change? When I call Tammer and ask her, "How's Don?" her answer is always, "The same." And no doubt she really means it. He is the same—yesterday, today, and I bet tomorrow too.

But even someone like Don, the poster child for being set in one's ways, changes every now and then. You and I change from time to time too. All humans do. That's because we are *mutable*, which means "changeable, variable, inconsistent, fluctuating, alterable." In fact, that definition right there is my testimony—I change *a lot*. I wish you could see this manuscript as I work on it. It is lit up like a Fourth of July sky with all the red edit marks from the track changes application! I change my word choice and I change my sentence placement. I change my mind and I change my opinion! My dear husband still can't understand why I change my handbags as often as I do. When it comes to food, fashion, home décor, and even my spiritual life, I'm the queen of mutable. And I think you and I may share that throne. In fact, the only thing that does not change about us is that we are changeable!

An Unchangeable God

All of us humans are prone to change, but not God. God is not mutable; he does not change. Throughout the Bible, there are passages that confirm God's immutability. Let's take a look at just four of them. (Unless I change my mind by the time I get to the fourth and add a fifth!)

1. In the Old Testament, a prophet named Balaam, who is trying to convince a pagan king that God is as good as his word,

makes this statement: "God is not human, that he should lie, not a human being, that he should change his mind. Does he speak and then not act? Does he promise and not fulfill? I have received a command to bless; he has blessed, and I cannot change it" (Numbers 23:19–20). What God says, he does. God does not change his word. It is immutable.

2. Many centuries later, another prophet named Malachi reminded the people of Israel that God's constancy and faithfulness were the only reasons they hadn't been destroyed. Through Malachi, God said, "'I the Lord do not change. So you, the descendants of Jacob, are not destroyed. Ever since the time of your ancestors you have turned away from my decrees and have not kept them. Return to me, and I will return to you,' says the Lord Almighty" (Malachi 3:6–7). The Lord stays true to his holy and merciful character, no matter what. His covenant is immutable. It does not change.

3. Now, fast-forward to the New Testament. The apostle Paul affirmed that God does not change when he wrote that "God's gifts and his call are irrevocable" (Romans 11:29). That means God doesn't renege on his commitments. God does not change his word, his standards, or his choices.

4. Lastly, James put it this way: "Every good and perfect gift is from above, coming down from the Father of the heavenly lights, who does not change like shifting shadows" (James 1:17).

Why am I making such a big deal about this characteristic of God? Why does it matter if God changes a teeny bit every once in a while? Can't that be OK since we trust him and know he is just in all his ways? It matters that God is immutable because if he could change, he would not be perfect. If he weren't perfect, then he would be like us—prone to error, fallible. How could we really trust a God like us?

Let me show you what I mean. Suppose you are on a championship curling team. (It could happen.) You and your three team-mates haven't yet lost a match playing this game of "chess" on ice. You all wield your brooms like the champs you are! You've had a perfect season, so you have a perfect record. Congratulations!

But suppose your amazing curling team had a perfect record, but it changed. What would that mean? Well, first of all it would mean that you may be tempted to break your broom handle and stomp off the ice in frozen fury! Why such severe reactions from you, the amazing curling champ, and your teammates? Because it would mean your curling team lost a match, thus marring your once pristine record. If something "perfect" changes, it can only change negatively.

So if a perfect God changes, what does he become?

Imperfect.

Uh ... *impossible*! If God changed through some type of modification, it would make him imperfect and incomplete. Yet the Bible is full of references that affirm the very opposite. To be perfect is to be complete, lacking nothing. To be complete is to be whole. God's nature is perfect and complete, and all that perfection and completeness coalesce in his holiness.

Perfectly Holy, Perfectly Whole

Now, why does God's holiness matter to you? When you're hurting and wondering why God is allowing pain in your life, getting a lesson on God's holiness is probably the furthest thing from your mind. But stay with me, and you will see why this matters. Verse after verse, God makes it pretty obvious that he wants you and me to understand he is holy. Here are just a few verses to affirm what I want you to see about him. Now, read these through because I promise this isn't just a Bible lesson! I want to tie together how God's immutability shows he is perfect and complete. And his completeness is captured in his holiness. And (deep breath) his holiness is the answer you need in your brokenness. Whew!

- God calls himself holy: "I, the LORD your God, am holy." (Leviticus 19:2)
- God says no one is holy like himself: "There is no one holy like the LORD." (1 Samuel 2:2)
- God, who inhabits all praise, is holy: "Yet you are enthroned as the Holy One; you are the one Israel praises." (Psalm 22:3)
- The holy God will show himself holy in righteousness: "The holy God will be proved holy by his righteous acts." (Isaiah 5:16)

See what I mean? God is pretty much saying, "This is not up for argument. I am holy. End of story." Yet, his holiness can be the beginning of your healing story. Here's why …

The Hebrew word from which we get our English word *holy* is *kadash*, which means "to hallow, to set apart, to sanctify." Because God is holy—complete and perfect—we should hallow his name and revere him. But it's also interesting that as our English language has evolved, *holy* has communicated a beautiful picture of our complete and holy God.

The English word *holy* comes from the Old English word *hālig*, a word related to *hāl*, which means "whole." The word *hāl* was used to convey the idea of uninjured, entire, or complete.

I love that because it affirms that God is complete, perfect, holy! How could *complete* change and become more complete? It can't. If *complete* changed, it would have to change to the negative, thereby becoming *incomplete.* God is holy and perfect. He is whole. He is complete and unchanging.

Because he is perfect, holy, and immutable, you can trust him. Even if you don't understand his ways, you can trust his character.

Because he is complete, you can find all you need in him. Embrace the holy God, and as you do, you will find your own wholeness. That's why we don't just take a part of God. That's why we don't create a God in our image, using only a few of his qualities and a few of our own. When you and I are willing to embrace the holiness of God, we embrace the "wholeness" of God. And when we really are willing to accept God in his wholeness, then, and only then, do we begin to experience our own wholeness.

Refusing to embrace the immutable, perfect, complete, holy, and whole character of God is refusing to receive the solution for our own brokenness. Because he is whole, you also can be, my friend. In him you have absolutely all you need for your whole life—and for a whole life.

(By the way, good luck on your next curling match!)

CHAPTER 8

Not the God We Expect

To fear God, is one of the first and greatest duties of his rational creatures.

Charles Inglis, *The Duty of Honouring the King*

During a dark spell of depression, I bought myself a necklace. Yes, retail therapy is a valid course of action. I've had times in my life when I'm sure I can prove that shopping is cheaper than therapy! Seriously though, this necklace wasn't an impulse buy or just a random act of retail. I sought this one out. My friend Angela helped me shop online for a pendant of Aslan.

Now, if you're not a totally obsessive C. S. Lewis lover like I am, you may not be familiar with The Chronicles of Narnia book series. So let me give you the gist of the story. Lewis created the great lion Aslan as a "supposal" of Christ. In other words, *suppose* there were another world and Christ visited it. Aslan, according to Lewis, is what he might be like. Aslan is wise and faithful, sacrificial and strong. He is good, the king of beasts, and son of the Emperor-beyond-the-Sea. I wanted a likeness of Aslan hanging around my neck to help me remember that Jesus was with me even in the depths of depression.

The necklace also helped me to remember one of my favorite quotes from *The Last Battle*, the final book in the series: "Courage, child: we are all between the paws of the true Aslan." I took comfort in remembering that Christ was my true Aslan and that my whole life was safe between his "paws," which I thought of as his outstretched, nail-scarred hands. But I also knew I was safe between the "pause" of the true Aslan. In other words, that dark time of depression when I questioned everything was like a pause God had either created or allowed in my life. And even though I was confused by it, that insecure place of pausing was also a place of safety because God doesn't make mistakes and I knew I could rest in him and trust his ways.

But that didn't and still doesn't mean I understand his ways! In fact, just when I think I kind of grasp a little of God and his ways, he surprises me. He acts in a way I didn't expect, or he doesn't act in a way I'd hoped he would. Just when I think I am figuring him out, I have reason to ask, "Who is he?" Have you felt that way? If so, it's OK because we are both in good company.

We aren't the first ones to find ourselves surprised, confused, and ultimately amazed by God. Those who knew Jesus best were also surprised. In a storm-tossed boat on the Sea of Galilee, Jesus' disciples just knew they were going to die. They feared for their lives and were not very happy to see Jesus asleep in the boat. They woke him with a stern reprimand: "Teacher, don't you care if we drown?" (Mark 4:38). Jesus got up and commanded the raging storm to calm down, and it did. With dropped jaws, the disciples looked at each other and asked, "Who is this? Even the wind and the waves obey him!" (Mark 4:41). Jesus was clearly not the God they expected. The psalmist had the same response when he considered his great God: "Who is he, this King of glory? The LORD Almighty—he is the King of glory" (Psalm 24:10).

When we truly begin to experience this God of mystery and love, we, too, should be overcome with awe and wonder. *Who is this God who cares so deeply for us, treats us justly, and is without error? Who is this God who keeps us safe between his "pause"?*

Who Is He?

When I really consider the question "Who is he?" my answers include, "He is good, kind, patient, faithful, intimately aware, comforting." And the list of his attributes could go on and on. Yet, though this King of glory is companionable and approachable, he is always to be feared—held in deep reverence—for he is the immutable, holy, complete, perfect God. Do you think it's possible to love God and fear God at the same time?

We are told to "love the LORD your God with all your heart and with all your soul and with all your strength" (Deuteronomy 6:5). Yet in the same Bible we are told, "The LORD Almighty is the one you are to regard as holy, he is the one you are to fear, he is the one you are to dread" (Isaiah 8:13).

Do those verses contradict each other? No. It is possible to both love and fear God. Not only is it possible; we are commanded to. But *fear* God? Why would we fear the God we love? If he is so caring and good, what is there to fear?

Look to Narnia

C. S. Lewis's Narnia may give us an imaginative insight into this paradox. In the first book of the Narnia series, *The Lion, the Witch and the Wardrobe*, the four Pevensie children find themselves in an imaginary world full of talking animals. Among the first Narnians they meet is a pair of beavers, who give them the lay of the land. When the children learn about Aslan, they detect from Mr. and Mrs. Beaver's comments and tone that Aslan must be quite a man. Then they're very surprised to find out he's not a man at all.

> "Ooh!" said Susan, "I'd thought he was a man. Is he—quite safe? I shall feel rather nervous about meeting a lion."
>
> "That you will, dearie, and no mistake," said Mrs. Beaver; "if there's anyone who can appear before Aslan without their knees knocking, they're either braver than most or else just silly."
>
> "Then he isn't safe?" said Lucy.
>
> "Safe?" said Mr. Beaver; "don't you hear what Mrs. Beaver tells you? Who said anything about safe? 'Course he isn't safe. But he's good. He's the King, I tell you."[*]

---

[*] C. S. Lewis, *The Lion, the Witch and the Wardrobe* (New York: Harper, 1950), 79–80.

The point Lewis is making is that goodness and safety are not the same thing when it comes to the King of glory. He is worthy of our fear. God himself said, "Fear your God. I am the LORD" (Leviticus 19:14). While fearing God includes reverence, the Hebrew word *yare* used in Leviticus 19:14 (and in numerous other Old Testament verses) literally means "fear" or "dread." For example, when God greeted Abram through a vision, he said, "Do not be afraid [*yare*], Abram. I am your shield, your very great reward" (Genesis 15:1).

And at the end of the Bible in the book of Revelation, when John is suddenly transported into Christ's presence, he describes it like this: "When I saw him, I fell at his feet as though dead. Then he placed his right hand on me and said: 'Do not be afraid. I am the First and the Last'" (Revelation 1:17).

If there is nothing to fear in the presence of the Lord—if his mere character evokes no trembling from us—why did God tell these men, who knew and loved God and who knew they were loved by God, not to fear? Don't miss the key point. God is a consuming fire. He is holy—both good and fierce.

When I was a girl, I loved my dad, and I knew how much he loved me. I had real respect for him. In fact, to this day, I have an almost reverent-like love for him. He has always been my hero, my rescuer, my teacher. As a child, he protected me, listened to me, and made me feel secure. He is a good, good man. But I can guarantee you this—as a girl, I did fear him. I knew he was capable of showing his authority and making my life miserable if he wanted to! He could spank me, send me to my room, or ground me. Part of the reason I obeyed him was that I loved and respected him, but part of the reason was also that I was plumb afraid of what he could do if I didn't!

I could love and fear my dad at the same time. I loved my father and had respect for his position. I had a healthy fear of his power. It is the same with God. We reverence and respect his position as the King of glory. We have a healthy fear of his power to create and destroy.

So who is this King who cares for us so deeply? He is the Lion of Judah, the King of kings. He may be the God we don't expect, but he is the God we need.

You may be living the questions, "God, do you care?" and "God, are you fair?" You may feel like your life has been put on hold by struggles and loss. But please know that you are between the "pause" of the good and holy Lion of Judah.

God himself may have allowed this deep time of sorrow for you so you can see him for the first time—I mean, see him for who he is, not just for who you thought he was or wished he was. He will hold you and carry you all your days. Keep asking him your questions. You are safe in his hands. He may not be the God you expect, but he will always be the God you need.

Jesus, I am resting, resting in the joy of what Thou art;
I am finding out the greatness of Thy loving heart.
Thou hast bid me gaze upon Thee, and Thy beauty fills my soul,
For by Thy transforming power Thou hast made me whole.

O, how great Thy loving kindness, vaster, broader than the sea!
O, how marvelous Thy goodness, lavished all on me!
Yes, I rest in Thee, Beloved, know what wealth of grace is Thine,
Know Thy certainty of promise, and have made it mine.

Simply trusting Thee, Lord Jesus, I behold Thee as Thou art,
And Thy love, so pure, so changeless, satisfies my heart,
Satisfies its deepest longings, meets, supplies its every need,
Compasseth me round with blessings, Thine is love indeed!

Jean Sophia Pigott, 1876

Threads of Truth for Your Blanket of Faith

- He is the Rock, his works are perfect, and all his ways are just. A faithful God who does no wrong, upright and just is he. (Deuteronomy 32:4)
- As for God, his way is perfect: The LORD's word is flawless; he shields all who take refuge in him. (Psalm 18:30)
- Our God is in heaven; he does whatever pleases him. (Psalm 115:3)
- "God is not human, that he should lie, not a human being, that he should change his mind. Does he speak and then not act? Does he promise and not fulfill?" (Numbers 23:19)
- "I am the LORD, and I do not change. That is why you descendants of Jacob are not already destroyed." (Malachi 3:6 NLT)
- "For my thoughts are not your thoughts, neither are your ways my ways," declares the LORD. "As the heavens are higher than the earth, so are my ways higher than your ways and my thoughts than your thoughts." (Isaiah 55:8–9)

Visit jenniferrothschild.com/threads to download free Scripture cards.

PART 3

God, Do You Hear Prayer?

I was sitting alone in my office, enveloped by the dark shadows of depression and feeling stifled by blindness. A cold February wind was rattling the windows, and the chill winds of doubt and confusion were rattling my heart. This was the beginning of a dark season. I felt lost in a fog with no bearings. And there was a question—one of many—that wouldn't let me go.

Why don't I truly ask God for healing?

As strange as it may sound, I was reluctant to pray for healing. I had learned long ago to seek God rather than healing, and in doing so I had learned to be content. Praying for healing—even allowing myself to *want* healing—was risky. I had worked too hard to become content, and I didn't want to shake up my world by exposing my tender heart to the pursuit of healing. Sometimes to hope is to hurt—and I was in enough pain already.

What if I pray for healing and God doesn't answer my prayer? How would I feel then? It's just easier to play it safe. I can't be disappointed in him if I don't give him a chance to disappoint me. But I do believe God can heal me. If I didn't, I wouldn't have consented to the requests of so many people over the years who asked to dab oil on my forehead and lay hands on me. And if I really weren't interested in healing, or if I thought God couldn't or wouldn't, I would never have let Phil put mud on my eyes.

It had happened so long ago. Phil and I were newlyweds. He went to the baseball field where he used to play shortstop in college—in South Florida, it was the only place we knew of that had mud. He took along an empty plastic bowl and returned with it full of wet, grimy clay. Earlier that week, I had received a letter from a stranger who had heard me speak. Based on Jesus' healing of the blind man in John 9, the letter writer felt God was prompting him on my behalf—if I put mud on my eyes and prayed in faith for healing, God would restore my sight.

Quite honestly, I rolled my eyes when Phil first read the letter. I don't like gimmicks or theatrics. But I couldn't stop thinking about it. *How do I know if and how God wants to heal me? What if God really is at work in this man's prompting?*

The more I thought about it, I realized that the real reason I didn't want mud on my eyes was pride. It was humiliating. Who wants dirty red clay smeared over their eyelids? But I also knew pride and unbelief don't invite healing, so I decided to let go of my pride and step out in faith.

Phil and I prayed earnestly as we stood in front of the bathroom sink, mud caked on both of my eyes. We said amen, and I washed off the clay in the sink. When I opened my eyes, they were still blind. I was disappointed but not surprised. Nor was I angry or discouraged. It was just one more in a long string of unanswered prayers for healing.

So, sitting in my office more than twenty-five years later, I tried to sort out the tangled mess of my conflicting thoughts and emotions. *Why should I pray for healing and put myself through something like that all over again? Is my desire to keep my sense of contentment just a thinly veiled attempt at self-protection? Is it self-centered not to pray for healing? Or perhaps the reason I don't pray for healing is that deep down I wonder if God will really hear me and answer me.*

God, do you hear prayer?

CHAPTER 9

Can You Even Hear Me?

Prayer is not asking. Prayer is putting oneself in the hands of God, at his disposition, and listening to his voice in the depth of our hearts.

Mother Teresa, *In My Own Words*

As I was in the guest room one night getting it ready for Easter guests, I turned on both lamps on the dresser. When I detected light from the right lamp but not the left, I put my hand on the bulb to make sure it was working. It was warm. If the lamp was on, the problem wasn't the lightbulb. My heart sank when it hit me. This could only mean one thing—the few fragments of sight I once had in my left eye were now gone. It's not like there was much vision there to begin with, but it was huge compared to the vast blackness of nothing at all. I suddenly felt trapped in a claustrophobic cave and overwhelmed by dread and loss. *I just can't believe I have no retina in my left eye. None. Blackness. I can't put into words how much I relied on the light perception I had in that eye. And now it's gone. Blackness. I hate it!*

My eyes welled up with tears and my throat got tight. "God, please give me back my left eye." I prayed out of sadness and desperation, not bitterness. I prayed because I knew God could restore even my limited sight. But should I have made a request rather than a demand? Would God hear a prayer that makes demands? Or was it OK to come boldly before the throne of grace in my time of need? Maybe my prayer was just an honest response to an honest loss in an honest relationship.

I poured out my grief and desperation. "Oh Father, I really want my left eye back. I don't even need total healing if you would just give me back the little light I had in my left eye. I feel such despair because I have just an island of light in my right eye. I had only small islands in my left eye, but they gave me such assistance in orientation."

The implications of the loss weighed so heavy, and then they got heavier still. "God, how long will it be until you take the light in my right eye? Please don't. Do you hear me, God? If healing is not your plan, I accept that. If you won't give me back my left eye, I will eventually accept that. But please do not take my right eye. I cannot accept that. I just can't. I trust you, I really do, but I want to tell you my heart. I dread the weariness that having no light in my left eye is ushering in. It is so tiring being blind. It wears me out. Life is wearing me out."

Can you identify with that kind of desperation? Have you ever begged God to change something or do something, while deep down you wondered if he even heard you? It's like being the guy on the cell phone commercials who's always asking, "Can you hear me now?" But the big question isn't really whether or not God *can* hear us, but whether or not he *does* hear us.

When we pray from the bottom of our souls, does God really tune in? If he does hear us, then why does it sometimes feel like he doesn't? Does he have selective hearing? You know, maybe God just tunes in for the prayers about the big things like hurricanes and world peace, but turns down the volume for the smaller prayers—like, "Help me remember what I studied as I take this test," or "Please give me a spouse, Lord," or "God, help this paycheck stretch until next Friday."

It's been nearly five years since I asked God to restore the limited sight in my left eye, and it remains as black as a starless midnight sky. Did God not hear my prayer? Did he tune in only to dismiss me? If Scripture teaches that God can and does hear, then maybe we're asking the wrong question. Maybe instead of asking "*Does* God hear?" we should be asking "*What* does God hear?"

What God Hears

The promise of Scripture is that God does hear us—and what he hears is the voice of our heart. The psalmist wrote, "In the morning, LORD, you hear my voice; in the morning I lay my requests before you and wait expectantly" (Psalm 5:3). The psalmist expresses the expectation that God hears his request clearly and knows exactly what he's prayed for. And that's how God hears you—crystal clear. Your voice isn't a vague noise from a distant room in heaven, like the voice of Charlie Brown's teacher, "Wah-wah-woh-wah-wah." God hears not only the words of your mouth, but even the unspoken utterances of your heart when you pray to him. He regards the specificity of your requests. He knows your voice and listens attentively to what you are saying. Just like parents can pick out their child's voice in a crowd, so God can hear your voice among the millions. He listens for it.

Not only does God hear your voice and what you're saying; he tunes in to your heartache when you suffer, and he longs to give you strength: "You, LORD, hear the desire of the afflicted; you encourage them, and you listen to their cry" (Psalm 10:17). God knows your heart. He hears what you say, and he knows what you mean. He created your heart, and he *gets* you. He knows what you want and need, and when he hears it, he immediately sends encouragement and strength your way.

On that day in the guest room when I prayed for God to heal my eye, he did hear my voice; I know he did. He regarded my sorrow, yet he did not restore the limited sight in my left eye. Still, I believe he heard my prayer because he did give me strength. God's encouragement for me came in the form of a renewed sense of security in my relationship with him and through the loyalty of friends who stuck with me while I was in such a low place.

Do you have a desire you long for God to hear?

"I need healing, Lord."

"God, please restore my marriage."

"Father, I feel so lonely. Please bring someone to love me."

God does hear your desire, my friend. Even if he hasn't answered it yet, that does not mean he disregards it. He hears you and he will move when and how it is best. Be strengthened and encouraged as you trust that God does hear you.

Who God Hears

In addition to what God hears, there is something else quite interesting in Scripture about *who* God hears. The psalmist writes, "The eyes of the LORD are on the righteous, and his ears are attentive to their cry" (Psalm 34:15).

God hears the prayers of the *righteous*? Uh-oh. Now, maybe that is my problem. I am the first to admit my motives and actions are often less than righteous. Perhaps you are grimacing right now because you don't think of yourself as righteous either. But consider what the Bible is really stating here.

The righteous aren't named as such because of their behavior. They are considered righteous because of their position. That means the righteous are not perfect; they are simply those who trust in God for their righteousness—they know God and are known by him. They aren't pious and perfect; they are simply made righteous by God's grace through faith in Jesus Christ. Righteousness is not achieved through our efforts but by receiving Christ as Savior. Think of it this way—God made us right with him. We have been brought into a right relationship with him. According to this understanding of righteous, I *am* righteous!

Jesus, the Righteous One

If we want to understand more about what it means that God hears the prayers of the righteous, there is no better example to turn to than *the* Righteous One, Jesus. He was the perfect Son of God—fully God, yet fully human. Just like you and me, he laid out his heart before his Father and prayed. Listen to how he prayed in Gethsemane: "He fell to the ground and prayed that if possible the hour might pass from him. '*Abba*, Father,' he said, 'everything is possible for you. Take this cup from me. Yet not what I will, but what you will'" (Mark 14:35–36).

Jesus prayed that if it was possible, this hour would pass from him. Now, let me ask you a question. Was it possible? Jesus knew it was possible because, as he stated, *all things* are possible with God. He knew God was listening, and he knew God could do

A Question of Righteousness

May I ask you a personal question? Are you one of "the righteous"? Do you have a relationship with God through Jesus Christ? Do you really know him, or do you just know about him? You may have gone to church, but that isn't the same as going to the cross and trusting Jesus for forgiveness and for a relationship with God.

I made that decision over thirty years ago, and it has changed my life forever. The only reason I can honestly deal with the mysteries of faith without totally falling apart is that I know God cares for me and loves me. I love how C. S. Lewis gives shape to this thought. He wrote, "I believe in Christianity as I believe that the sun has risen: not only because I see it, but because by it I see everything else."*

I may not understand all the paradox and mystery of Christianity, but I know its truth because of how it has sustained me and given meaning and illumination to everything in my life. I know Jesus Christ is real, and he has saved me and brought me into a place of peace. I want that for you too. Put simply, have you received Christ's gift of grace?

My friend, if you haven't, I invite you to trust Jesus Christ as your Savior. "If you declare with your mouth, 'Jesus is Lord,' and believe in your heart that God raised him from the dead, you will be saved. For it is with your heart that you believe and are justified, and it is with your mouth that you profess your faith and are saved" (Romans 10:9–10). If you have just become a Christian, or if you want to become a Christian, tell someone you know who is a Christian so they can help you. Or e-mail me. I would love to connect you with people who love Christ and will love you too!

---

*C. S. Lewis, *The Weight of Glory and Other Addresses* (New York: HarperCollins, 2001), 140.

anything. So he prayed, and he asked. When our hearts are full of sorrow or fear, we can't help but throw ourselves at God's feet and pray because we know all things are possible with God.

Although Jesus knew all things were possible with God, he also knew his mission was to give his life as a ransom for sinners (Mark 10:45). In other words, he knew God's will for his life. And knowing the Father's will, Jesus still asked to be spared.

What are your thoughts about what Jesus did? Pause here for a moment and allow me to tell you another story about our oldest son, Clayton, to help you consider this issue from another perspective.

When Clayton was still in elementary school, every week I asked the family, "What do you need from the store?" The typical responses were things like "I need deodorant" or "We're low on cereal." The requests varied each week, except for one very predictable response from Clayton. With a silly grin on his face, he'd say, "I want a Nintendo 64." Every week for a solid year he made the same request, and every week I laughed. He wanted that gaming system, and he knew I had the means to get it for him. Although it was possible for me to buy it, what was possible was not the deciding factor. Clayton knew we didn't just spend hundreds of dollars whenever we wanted to, as if the money popped out of our printer every time we pressed a magic key. Phil and I were saving such a gift for his birthday, and deep down, Clayton probably knew that. He knew the deciding factor wasn't his desire or our financial liquidity. The deciding factor rested with his mother—her will. Even though Clayton knew my will concerning the N64, he asked anyway. His request was simply a way to tell me the desire of his heart.

Now, keep that story in mind as we go back to Gethsemane. Jesus knew it was possible for God to change things, but he also knew his Father's will. Jesus expressed the deep anguish of his heart to his Father. He cried out to his *Abba*—the Aramaic word for "daddy." He pressed into his Dad's heart and poured out all his emotion in God's presence. He knew anything was theoretically possible with God; yet he also knew that ultimately the Father's will would prevail. So why did he bother to pray?

I wonder if Jesus prayed that prayer as much for our sake as for his. As a human being, sweat pouring off him like drops of blood, he certainly longed for another way to fulfill God's will. He wanted the cup of suffering to pass, even though he knew it was his to drink. Yet perhaps he prayed as he did in part to show us how we can pray to our Father with our hearts wide open. Because God does hear our voices, and he hears the desires of those who suffer, Jesus gave the example of what to do with our deepest longings when we are suffering. We can appeal to God about anything because with him all things are possible and he hears us. But perhaps there is still another reason Jesus prayed that prayer. Maybe it was to show us the difference between what is *possible* and what is *best*.

What Is Possible versus What Is Best

What if the cup of suffering had passed from Jesus? The results would have been a relief for him, but they would have been eternally disastrous for us. Even though it was possible for God to change things, ultimately it was not what he deemed best.

I know it is possible for God to restore those tiny patches of retina that were in my left eye. I know he can put a hold on that tiny island of retina that remains in my right eye. Shoot, he can just heal both my eyes and make them 20/20 if he wants to. And, as Crystal Gayle once sang, he could even "make my brown eyes blue." Anything is possible with God. And yet, for now at least, I surrender myself to the fact that it is not what he deems best. And perhaps the same is true for you. It is entirely possible that God will answer the deepest prayer of your heart for healing or deliverance or provision. All things are possible with God. But it may also be that what is possible is not what God deems best.

Jesus ended his prayer in obedient surrender: "Not what I will, but what you will" (Mark 14:36). After expressing his desires, Jesus ultimately prayed not just for what was possible but for what God deemed best. He prayed for God's will to be done instead of his own will.

That's really hard sometimes, isn't it? My will is for my friend's cancer to go away. My will is for my friend's son's drug addiction to vanish. Those things are possible with God. And they may in fact be his will—and I pray as if those requests *are* his will. I know he can accomplish these things in the lives of people I care about. But ultimately, I trust God's will to be best. He knows more, sees more, and loves more than I do.

How do you pray most of the time? Be honest. Do you pray for your will, or do you routinely surrender yourself to God's will? When you really trust your *Abba* and focus on his will, you are empowered to pray for what is best, not merely for what is possible. If you pray for his will, it is guaranteed that God hears your prayer. That is the promise of Scripture: "This is the confidence we have in approaching God: that if we ask anything according to his will, he hears us" (1 John 5:14).

Since we know God *can* hear us and that he *does* hear us, if he does not answer in the time or way we hope, it doesn't mean he isn't listening. When we pray, we lift up our need and willingly accept his will in response. As hard as it is for me to admit this, what is best for me is God's will. For now, that means I am blind. My will—what I want and think is best—is limited and unreliable. And so I surrender to what God deems best, even as I continue to pour out my heart to him about my needs.

For you and me, to pray for what is best for us and the people we love is to pray for God's will. Let us not settle for merely what is possible; let us reach in prayer for what is best.

My friend, God cares about you. He cares enough to hear; he cares enough to listen; and he cares enough about you not to let you settle for what is possible. He lovingly invites you to pray for his will because the center of his will is the safest place you could ever be. What is possible may be good, but it may not be what is best. Are you willing to pray like Jesus? Are you willing to appeal to God's power, yet yield to his will? Through God's grace, let us learn to be willing.

CHAPTER 10

God, If You're Listening, Make a Move!

*Our struggle is—isn't it?—to achieve and retain faith on a
lower level ... Even to go on believing that there is a Listener
at all. For as the situation grows more and more desperate,
the grisly fears intrude. Are we only talking to ourselves in an
empty universe? The silence is often so emphatic. And we have
prayed so much already.*

C. S. Lewis, *Letters to Malcolm*

My parents raised my two brothers and me in a tiny house in
Miami, Florida. It didn't seem tiny until I grew up and realized all five of us humans and one dog were crammed into fifteen
hundred square feet. But most of the time the size of our house was
no big deal because we kids were always outside playing kickball
or swimming. The backyard pool was definitely the best feature of
our house. The previous owners had the builders put in a two-foot
square tile chessboard in the shallowest end of the pool, which was
about a foot under water. It came with stout, sand-filled chessmen,
each about six inches tall, that stood like chubby sentinels guarding the shallow end. A few of the pawns that had served double
duty as chew toys for the dog were scratched, but other than that,
the pieces were perfect. It was novel and fun, and so I learned to
play chess!

My most vivid memories of pool chess are the games I played
against my brother David. Although he was almost ten years

younger, he always beat me—or I gave up before he had a chance to. I approached chess like a hundred-yard dash, and he approached it like a marathon. He took his time, studied the board, and thought about strategy. His big sister moved the first piece she touched. When I impatiently told him to hurry up, he just sat there staring at the board, apparently not listening to me at all. If I forfeited the game before his strategy unfolded, we simply tossed the pawns into the deep end and dove in after them. David thought ahead and was slow to move; I couldn't see any further than the next move and was impulsive. He was about the whole board; I was about one piece. Maybe you can see where I'm headed with this story.

I think our lives with God feel something like this from time to time. We sit on one side of the chessboard of life, focused only on what's right in front of us and hoping one or two quick moves get us to the other side of the difficulty we face. We wait for God to make a move in response to our nudging in prayer. We ask him to please hurry up and do something, but it often feels like our requests fall on very distracted ears. Is it only me, or do you sometimes feel like God's stillness means he isn't doing anything?

That's how my friend Stacy must have felt in the fall of 2012. For two weeks, she and her family and friends prayed diligently for her husband, Matt. What started out as severe flu-like symptoms quickly led to unconsciousness. Doctors discovered a staph infection but couldn't determine why Matt was losing consciousness or why he had a mass on his kidney and an infection in his heart.

Every prayer we lifted from the waiting room of the intensive care unit was met by more questions rather than answers. Prayers for improvement were followed by no change at all or by a change for the worse. It seemed like God just wasn't moving in the way or at the pace Matt needed him to. All we wanted to see in response to our prayers was a move forward from God—just one tiny move so we would know he was in the game with us. If Matt would just open his eyes or squeeze Stacy's hand. If he would just offer a grin when he heard his mother's voice ... if Matt would just do anything encouraging, we would have received it as movement from God.

But Matt continued to deteriorate, despite the fact that the hospital waiting room was full of praying people. Why didn't God move?

"Oh, That You Would ..." Prayers

We live in a culture accustomed to instant gratification. Fast food, one-click shopping, overnight shipping. We are what I call "*if/then* oriented." You know, *if* I order, *then* I get my burger. *If* I click send, *then* I get an instant e-mail confirmation. So it's hard to disregard that mind-set when it comes to prayer. *If* I ask, *then* God moves.

The prophet Isaiah gave voice to what it feels like when we want to see something—anything—from God so we know he is active on our behalf:

> *Oh, that you would rend the heavens and come down,*
>   *that the mountains would tremble before you!*
> *As when fire sets twigs ablaze*
>   *and causes water to boil,*
> *come down to make your name known to your enemies*
>   *and cause the nations to quake before you!*
> *For when you did awesome things that we did not expect,*
>   *you came down, and the mountains trembled before you.*
> *Since ancient times no one has heard,*
>   *no ear has perceived,*
> *no eye has seen any God besides you,*
>   *who acts on behalf of those who wait for him.*
>
> Isaiah 64:1–4

Isaiah prayed an "Oh, that you would ..." prayer. He cried out to God, asking him to move, to do something. He needed affirmation that God was listening, and he thought that if God took some initiative, Israel's enemies would also know that God was in the game. If the sky suddenly ripped open, mountains started to jiggle like Jell-O, and God came down, Isaiah would surely know that God was listening and active, wouldn't he?

Sometimes we do our own version of the Isaiah plea: "Oh, that you would make this house sell." "Oh, that you would make the test results negative." "Oh, that you would steer this storm away from our town." We know how that feels, don't we? If the roof lifted from above you as you were praying and God rained down thousands of ten-dollar bills in response to your prayer for provision, you'd be pretty convinced God was in the game, right? If Matt sat up in bed and called out for Stacy while we were praying, I would certainly have known God was listening to our prayers. But is instant response the only way we can know God is listening to us and is active on our behalf?

Instant response is an obvious way we know God is listening, but it isn't the only way we know he is listening. The longer I've walked with God and the more I've met him in prayer, I've come to believe the only way to really know God is listening to our prayers is by faith. Yes, faith is truly the only way we know God hears and is listening. He says he is listening, and we have to trust he is. Faith is the evidence of things unseen; instant response is not the evidence. I know that isn't an easy answer, but it is the true answer.

Faith allows us to see that God does sometimes choose to answer obviously and speedily, but just as often, he chooses to answer slowly and invisibly. And when we've prayed our "Oh, that you would ..." prayers for a while, our prayers can take on a different vocabulary. We begin to pray, "How long, Lord?" We wonder how long we will have to wait for his answer.

"How Long?" Prayers

Habakkuk was a prophet in Judah in the late seventh century BC. When his country was entangled in evil and corruption, he called out to God to make a move. Jehoiakim, the king, was ungodly and rebellious (2 Kings 23:36–24:7; 2 Chronicles 36:5–8). Shortly after Jehoiakim came to power, Habakkuk penned his lament over the violence, wickedness, and greed that surrounded him: "How long, LORD, must I call for help, but you do not listen?" (Habakkuk 1:2). Habakkuk essentially said, "God, why don't you do something? Why don't you make a move? Why aren't you listening?"

When you pray "How long?" prayers, perhaps you also wonder if God is listening to you. I know I have felt that way and wondered how much longer I would have to hold on before God moved. At one particularly low point, I wrote this "How long?" prayer in my journal:

> *What is wrong with me? This despair is too much. Is this chemical? Could meds help balance me a little? Is this aging? Is this just the toll of blindness? Has it seemed easier for years because I was younger?*
>
> *Oh, God, you must help me. I am not asking for a fix. I need help. Are you ever going to heal me here on earth? If so, right now would be good. I don't think you are. This may be my life. Make me spiritually peaceful then.*
>
> *I always suggest blindness is a friend. Tonight, it's not. It is an unwelcome invader that is stealing everything that matters to me. I feel beat up by it, a victim of it, and hopeless to fight back and win. Hopeless. When will something give? God, how long will it be this way?*
>
> *God, help me. I am dying in this. I do not want to live the rest of my days stuck in a blind body.*

When I wrote that entry, I was about nine months deep into depression, even though I didn't know it. After a devastating experience at a speaking engagement, I was on an airplane headed for home, and all I wanted was to disappear. I had gotten disoriented on stage. It wasn't the first time, but it was the final time—you know, the proverbial straw that broke the camel's back. I had tried to laugh it off, but inside I was terrified. I couldn't concentrate—and I couldn't remember how many steps I had taken in what direction, so I ended up speaking to the right side of the stage rather than to the audience.

I knew something was seriously wrong and that I had to get help. When I finally went to see a doctor, I discovered I was in full-blown menopause. My brain chemistry and female hormones had all split! I learned the hard lesson that when blindness meets menopause, let's just say they don't play nice. The result was depression, and it lasted far longer than I expected. I prayed many "How long?" prayers: "How long, Lord, will I be in this low place, with no energy and ability to do life?"

When we pray a Habakkuk-like "How long?" prayer, it is often accompanied by an Isaiah-like "Oh, that you would ..." prayer. For me, it was "Oh, that you would just pull me out of this pit!" "How long will I stumble along in my own personal darkness?" "Oh, that you would do something, Lord, to give me just a little hope that I won't always feel like this."

What is your "How long?" prayer? What is your "Oh, that you would ..." prayer? Has God answered those prayers? Do you think he is listening? My friend, God is listening, and he does hear you. He heard Habakkuk too, and he answered. If you read Habakkuk 1:5–11, you'll see that God not only listened; he answered.

God told Habakkuk he was about to make a move that would utterly amaze Habakkuk. Isn't that just like God? While we are crying out, "How long?" and "Oh, that you would ..." prayers, wondering if he is even listening, God is already in the process of answering our prayers. We find ourselves impatiently waiting for the next move as a sign that God is in the game, when he is already busy strategizing and moving his game plan along.

Now, let me be painfully clear. When God told Habakkuk he would be amazed, God wasn't referring to the kind of "amazed" we might feel when we get a big diamond ring or a new car. God was answering Habakkuk's "How long?" prayer with an excruciating answer. He was moving the ruthless Babylonian army into position to attack Habakkuk's people (Habakkuk 1:6). The answer was severe, but the result would be right.

God finally did make a move we recognized for our friend Matt—and it, too, was an excruciating answer. God chose to take him home. That wasn't what we were praying for, but that is how God answered. It wasn't until many days later that we learned Matt had renal cancer. God was listening, moving, and seeing the whole board, acting on Matt's behalf for Matt's good.

We can't see how the game will play out, and so we tend to pray one-move-at-a-time kind of prayers. Does that mean we shouldn't bother praying? No, the Bible tells us that "the prayer of a righteous person is powerful and effective" (James 5:16). In other words, our prayers make a difference. When Abraham prayed that God would not destroy Sodom, he fervently appealed, "What if there are fifty righteous people?" all the way down to "What if only ten can be found there?" Abraham's fervent prayer was powerful and effective. God agreed to forbear according to each of Abraham's appeals rather than immediately destroy the city as he said (Genesis 18:16–33).

Sometimes our prayers do get an instant response from God. And for those answers we are so very grateful. Other times, our prayers don't seem to make any difference at all. Regardless of the outcome, your prayers will always make a difference in your heart. As the poet James Dillet Freeman wrote, "Sometimes the answer to prayer is not that it changes life, but that it changes you." As you seek confirmation that God is tuned in, you will become tuned to his heart. When you meet God in prayer, you cannot help but be changed. He softens your heart, strengthens your faith, and lavishes you with his love when you are in his presence. As your heart is changed through connecting with your heavenly Father in prayer, you will find you can rest in his strategic inactivity. So, my friend, it's your move—take a step of faith and wait on God.

CHAPTER 11

Good God, Lousy Answers

Every war, every famine or plague, almost every death-bed, is the monument to a petition that was not granted.

C. S. Lewis, *Letters to Malcolm*

Unanswered prayer is a perplexing spiritual issue, especially in light of the audacious promises in the Bible. Jesus stated simply, "Ask and it will be given to you" (Luke 11:9). Speaking through the psalmist, God stated, "He will call on me, and I will answer him" (Psalm 91:15). Finally, a formula! We ask; God answers. Done. Next ...

I wish.

You know as well as I do that it isn't that simple, even though it seems like it should be. Why is that? God isn't lying. We aren't confused—or could we be? God says he will answer us when we pray. I believe him. So perhaps what we sometimes think is no answer really is an answer. It's just what we consider a *bad* answer.

Bad Answers?

In eighth grade, my classmate Alex Rodriguez had a Christmas stocking full of chocolate Hershey Kisses in his desk. He had been handing them out during homeroom that December morning. For whatever reason, he hadn't given me one—and I wanted that chocolate! So I leaned toward him from my desk one aisle over and whispered rather loudly, "Can I have a Kiss?" Before I knew what happened, a pair of puffy, wet adolescent lips were planted on mine! I jerked back, sitting upright in my chair, and gave him the dirtiest look I could muster while kids around us laughed. "You know what I meant!" I scolded. He proudly chuckled, "You asked me for a kiss. I gave you one. I don't know what you're so mad about." What a knucklehead! To make matters worse, I never even got the Hershey Kiss! (It still makes me mad when I think about it.) Alex answered me, didn't he? He didn't ignore me or disregard me. He listened and answered. It just wasn't the answer I expected.

Sometimes it feels like that is what happens with God too. Because he promises, we expect a response from him. But what we expect is a good answer, not a lousy one. And there's even biblical support for that expectation from Jesus himself:

> *Which of you, if your son asks for bread, will give him a stone? Or if he asks for a fish, will give him a snake? If you, then, though you are evil, know how to give good gifts to your children, how much more will your Father in heaven give good gifts to those who ask him!*
>
> Matthew 7:9–11

Jesus describes God as a father in this passage and contrasts God's goodness to "evil" parents. Now, don't let his "evil" adjective trip you up. He isn't saying that earthly parents are sinister, but he is acknowledging human sinfulness. Jesus uses an extreme comparison to contrast our capacity for goodness, even though we are sinful, compared to God's capacity for goodness when he is wholly good. Compared to his goodness, we might as well be described as evil. The point he is making is that if fallen, flawed human beings want to give their very best to their children, then how much more does God want to do the same?

Our Father God is good and doesn't engage in bait-and-switch tactics — we don't ask him for daily bread only to receive stones instead. Still, it doesn't always feel like his answers are good ones.

What are we to do when we experience lousy answers? If God promises to give us what is good, then why do we end up with what sometimes seems more like the snake Jesus mentions? Healing from cancer is good, yet people die from the disease with prayers for healing on their lips. Surviving a car wreck is good, yet I've attended one too many funerals of young people who have been killed behind the wheel. We pray for healing from cancer and for protection for our children on the road. God promises good gifts when we ask—yet it seems we too often end up with something we don't want instead. How can we reconcile God's promise of giving good gifts with the reality of lousy answers to prayer?

Remember the prophet Habakkuk from the last chapter? His story has helped me navigate this conundrum of lousy answers to prayer. You'll recall that Habakkuk was grieved and perplexed that God seemingly did nothing about wickedness and oppression running rampant in Judah. He prayed "How long?" prayers, urging God to move. When he was told that the Lord was preparing to do something about it through the ruthless Babylonians (Habakkuk 1:6), his confusion only grew. How could God, who is "too pure to look on evil," appoint such a nation "to execute judgment" on a people "more righteous than themselves" (Habakkuk 1:12, 13)?

You have to admit, God's answer to Habakkuk's "How long?" prayer was lousy. Habakkuk's people were to be taken captive and their land destroyed—by the unholy Babylonians, no less. When Habakkuk prayed, the inevitable attack from the Babylonians must have felt like a snaky answer rather than the fishlike response he hoped for. What a hard provision.

God also made it clear, however, that eventually the corrupt Babylonians would themselves be destroyed. At the end of the day, Habakkuk learned to rest in God's will and patiently wait for God to do what God deemed best. Habakkuk realized that because God is good, the result of prayer is always good—even when the answer seems lousy.

Have you ever asked your heavenly Father for a loaf of bread and felt like you got a bag of rocks instead? You know, like asking

God to help you earn a promotion at work and instead you get fired? How could what you think is bad really be good?

Good Gifts

I thought God handed me a bunch of rocks and a snake when Phil and I moved to a new community and a new church. I had recorded a couple of CDs and had been traveling and singing. Our new church knew this, yet they rarely asked me to sing. I grew more curious and frustrated as the months turned into a year. I prayed, wondering why God wasn't opening that door; after all, singing was my gift and my ministry.

At the same time, Phil was asked to lead a college Bible study and asked me to team teach it with him. I had never taught before. I found the experience challenging, and each week I taught, I experienced God revealing a gift I didn't know I had. The more I taught, the more passionate I became about teaching. God graciously declined my plea to share in the music ministry because he wanted to give me time to grow in teaching. What I thought was a snaky answer was really a life-giving fish in disguise.

Unanswered prayer and prayers with disappointing answers can be greater gifts than getting what we thought we wanted. Scripture reminds us that God's ways are not always our ways. "'My thoughts are not your thoughts, neither are your ways my ways,' declares the LORD. 'As the heavens are higher than the earth, so are my ways higher than your ways and my thoughts than your thoughts'" (Isaiah 55:8–9). You and I need to beware of prayer that limits and confines God simply because we are convinced that we know what is best. God's "unanswered" prayer may be the greater gift!

Even what we consider bad answers to our prayers can be the best answer. The answer may seem bad because it stings like a snake or injures like a rock, but when we look back, we will see they were fish and bread in disguise because they nourished and grew us.

Are you dealing with snakes or rocks right now, wondering why God didn't give the "good gifts" he promised? Can you see those snakes and rocks as the good gifts God promised? Can you see them as fish and bread? Is God using them to grow you? To nourish you? My friend, if God only gives good gifts, then could what you are dealing with really be just a fish in snake's clothing?

Consider this: God does not capriciously give us what feels like snakes and rocks. What he gives to us he grants for a deeper purpose—a purpose that includes far more than just our immediate comfort, relief, or personal gain. So even if it feels like snakes and stones, treat it like the fish and bread it is. You will grow deeper in faith as a result of disappointment. You will be wiser, gentler, and more empathetic as a result of your personal pain. God gives good gifts—always.

CHAPTER 12

The Ultimate Answer

"God, if Thou dost never answer another prayer while I live on this earth, I will still worship Thee as long as I live and in the ages to come for what Thou hast done already." God's already put me so far in debt that if I were to live one million millenniums I couldn't pay him for what he's done for me.

A. W. Tozer, *Essays on Prayer*

I really don't think God plays favorites when it comes to football," the cranky guy snorted over his shoulder from the bleacher in front of us. At least he waited for my friend Andréa to say the amen of her prayer before making his big doctrinal pronouncement.

"I know, I know," Andréa apologetically conceded. "We just can't afford to lose this game!" My interest was piqued as I sat quietly listening to her and Mr. Cranky engage in a theological discussion about prayer and football.

A bunch of us middle-aged moms had gathered to watch our friend's son play football. We happened to be sitting on the home team side, even though we were rooting for the visiting team. I guess that's why Mr. Cranky was so annoyed. If we were going to appeal to God for a win, it should at least be for his team. Truth be told, I wasn't too excited about the game, but I was totally pumped that the doctrinal sparks were flying. Talk about an interesting matchup—Crusty Cranky versus Angelic Andréa!

Was Mr. Cranky right? Does God disregard prayers for things like football games? Or does he stop what he is doing in heaven when you ask him for a parking space? If he does hear these prayers, does he respond with an answer? You know, like if enough people pray for the red team, will God say, "OK, the red team wins today"? Or if there's a shiny blue minivan headed for the parking spot you want, will God do a cosmic sleight of hand so you can get there first instead?

Now, before you think I'm as cranky as Mr. Cranky, let me share this. When I was a college student, a well-known Christian singer came to our university to perform. His music was totally inspiring and engaging. After a few songs, he shared how he'd noticed that Christian dance clubs were beginning to pop up around the country. Of course, all the college students erupted in applause, and a chorus of whoops filled the arena.

We were abruptly stopped, however, when the performer interrupted our cheer with scolding: "Don't you know there are people dying and going to hell, children starving, and all the while, Christians are *dancing*?" It took a moment for us to realize he was serious and seriously miffed at our clapping. He then proceeded to shame us for even considering the notion of dancing when people in the world were suffering.

Ouch. (Mr. Cranky must have a twin.)

The rest of the concert felt more like being grounded or sent to our rooms without supper. I felt like a Christian brother slapped our hands, sucked the joy out of our faith, and rained judgment down on us all. I share this story because I don't want what you are about to read to make you feel like I did that night. I just want us to explore this honestly. And I know you may have prayed for a football win or an empty parking spot before. (I have!)

Andréa's heart was pure when she appealed to God for the football win. God heard her, and I bet he even smiled. I'm not condemning the content of anyone's prayer. And I am not scolding anyone. I promise. I just want us to honestly consider what God hears when we pray.

The Promise of Good Gifts

Jesus himself tells us to ask, seek, and knock in prayer. The result? If we ask, we receive. If we seek, we find. If we knock, the door swings open (Matthew 7:7–8). Does that mean we can ask, seek, and knock about things like football games and expect to get answers from God? After all, Jesus tells us that if earthly parents, who are sinful, give good gifts to their children, "how much more will your Father in heaven give *good gifts* to those who ask him!" (Matthew 7:11, emphasis added).

The two Greek words translated "good gifts" are *domata agatha*, a plural noun form, which tells us that God intends to give us more than one good gift. What could those gifts possibly be? Football wins? An empty parking place near the door when it's raining? Fish sticks and breadsticks rather than snakes and rocks? What about healing from cancer or a financial rescue? What does "good gifts" mean?

If we look at the context of Jesus' words in Matthew 6 and 7, we find good gifts connected to choices and actions that develop character. God's good gifts lead us to give, pray, forgive, fast, store up treasure in heaven, refrain from worry, and pursue wisdom. So perhaps the good gifts Jesus refers to are spiritual. If we seek those good things, we will find them; if we knock on their doors, those doors will swing open so we can walk through them by faith. These good things are gifts from our Father in heaven. He will never withhold these good gifts when we ask him.

Now friend, that doesn't mean God answers only prayers concerning spiritual things, but it does make me pay attention to what I'm praying for. What is my motive? Am I totally earthbound or self-centered in my praying? What is my ultimate goal in prayer? How about you?

The "good gifts" the disciple Matthew describes in broad terms are pinpointed more specifically by Dr. Luke. Here's how he quotes Jesus: "If you then, though you are evil, know how to give good gifts to your children, how much more will your Father in heaven give the Holy Spirit to those who ask him!" (Luke 11:13).

Jesus says that the ultimate good gift God gives to those who ask is the gift of the Holy Spirit. The gift of the Holy Spirit is *the* good gift—the ultimate response to our prayers. The Holy Spirit is our Comforter, our Helper, our Companion, and the One who teaches and guides us into truth (John 14:16–18, 26). His presence is more comforting and satisfying than any other answer we could receive from God.

Content and Satisfied with God

I think the prophet Habakkuk must have understood this truth that the Holy Spirit is the ultimate good gift. After Habakkuk prayed, "How long?" God gave him an answer that was hard to hear. But Habakkuk's response was surprisingly content: "Though the fig tree does not bud and there are no grapes on the vines, though the olive crop fails and the fields produce no food, though there are no sheep in the pen and no cattle in the stalls, yet I will rejoice in the LORD, I will be joyful in God my Savior" (Habakkuk 3:17–18).

The prophet Habakkuk wrote those contented words though he knew the land of Judah would soon be attacked by the Babylonians, the land decimated, the crops destroyed. Yet, Habakkuk did not rail at God's cruelty or doubt God's love. He wasn't cranky or harsh. He was satisfied. He was satisfied even though his prayers got a lousy answer.

Can you say the same? If not, would you like to feel that way? I would. Who wants to go through life like Mr. Cranky—bitter and discontent when things don't work out like we want them to? Wouldn't we all prefer to be restful and at peace?

My friend, the reason Habakkuk was satisfied—the reason you and I can be satisfied, no matter what answer we receive—is that God gives the good gift of himself to each of us as the ultimate answer to our prayer. Satisfaction doesn't come only from answers to our prayers. Satisfaction comes from the encounter we have with God through his Spirit because of our prayer. Answers never fully satisfy—only a relationship with God satisfies.

God's ultimate answer to your prayers is the good gift of the Holy Spirit. He is the affirmation that God is with you. Because of the Holy Spirit, you know God listens to you, hears your concerns, and answers well. Don't settle for lesser gifts and smaller answers when it comes to prayer.

Oh, and P.S., our football team lost! Score one for Mr. Cranky and his boys.

CHAPTER 13

Jesus Had an Unanswered Prayer Too

"My God, my God, why have you forsaken me?"

Matthew 27:46

If you wonder about the problem of unanswered prayer, you are in the best possible company. When Jesus cried out from the cross, "My God, my God, why have you forsaken me?" he was calling out to God, but he heard no answer. Did you ever think of that? Jesus knows how it feels when God doesn't answer an anguished, heartfelt prayer. Jesus knows what it's like to feel abandoned by God because he is silent when you most need to hear his voice.

According to Scripture, it was three in the afternoon when Jesus called out to heaven. Exhausted by torture and despair, he was physically weak, emotionally spent, and spiritually devastated. Given his depleted state, Jesus could have whispered his question from the cross, but both Matthew and Mark (Mark 15:34) record that he shouted it.

When we find ourselves on a cross in our lives—a place in which we feel pain, confusion, or darkness—we want to shout to God, "Why have you forsaken me? God, why have you left me here in this sorrow with no word from you?" We pray because we need clarity in our darkness. Sometimes we pray because we need to hear God's voice reassuring us. Almost always we pray because we genuinely want an answer. *God, where are you?*

Jesus already knew the answer to the question he asked from the cross. From the beginning of time, he knew he would be forsaken by his Father when he took on our sins. According to Scripture, God made Jesus Christ, "who had no sin *to be sin* for us, so that in him we might become the righteousness of God" (2 Corinthians 5:21, emphasis added). In other words, God put our sins on Christ. Christ took on our sin and, in turn, made us righteous.

This is the way the apostle Paul explains the impact of Christ's death on the cross:

> *Our firm decision is to work from this focused center: One man died for everyone. That puts everyone in the same boat. He included everyone in his death so that everyone could also be included in his life, a resurrection life, a far better life than people ever lived on their own...*
>
> *Anyone united with the Messiah gets a fresh start, is created new. The old life is gone; a new life burgeons! Look at it! All this comes from the God who settled the relationship between us and him, and then called us to settle our relationships with each other. God put the world square with himself through the Messiah, giving the world a fresh start by offering forgiveness of sins ... Become friends with God; he's already a friend with you.*
>
> *How? you ask. In Christ. God put the wrong on him who never did anything wrong, so we could be put right with God.*
>
> 2 Corinthians 5:14–15, 17–21 MSG

It's a divine mystery, but the Bible tells us that all of our sins — your sin, my sin, Hitler's sin, your grandma's sin — was placed on Jesus. The perfect Son of God absorbed all the ugliness, shame, and torment of our sin. Because Jesus *became* sin for us, God had to forsake him — he could not look upon sin. God had to abandon Jesus in order to never abandon you. Sin separates us from God. Jesus bore the pain of that separation for us so we wouldn't have to.

Silence from heaven was the only response a just God could give to Jesus as he bore our sin. Jesus knew that. In his omniscience, he knew that the silence of God during that dark hour was evidence of God's faithfulness. For in the wrath of God on Jesus was the fulfillment of God's plan. Jesus knew intellectually that God had forsaken him at that moment in order to remain faithful to his plan and character. Yet he still asked the question. Jesus didn't struggle with a theological misunderstanding or paternal abandonment. He was confronted by the tangled emotions that slay us when we suffer. In his humanity, he felt as devastated by abandonment as we do.

What a stunning example Jesus set for us even in his death! He gave us permission to ask questions. He showed us that even in a dark and difficult moment, we can recognize in some mysterious way that God's will still makes sense. He proved that it is possible to choose a cross—to give our consent to God even in the midst of something that is tearing us up. And he showed that even when we're intellectually and spiritually intact, we can still struggle with the difficult emotions that often show up as questions when we suffer.

- *"God, why didn't you answer me? Now I'm alone in this empty, foreclosed house that used to be my home."*
- *"Jesus, please heal my child. Make this medicine work. Please, Lord."*
- *"Lord, when will this depression lift? Why won't you give me an answer?"*

Often our prayers are a way to corral our emotions to keep them from crushing our hearts. We would like an answer from God. But even more than an answer, we need to know he hears us and cares. I can't imagine how Jesus must have felt that day on the cross. The weight of our sin and his physical torment must have been excruciating all by themselves. But knowing he had been abandoned by God must have been unbearable. Why couldn't God have simply whispered from heaven, "I am here. I just have to be quiet. This will be over soon." God could have spoken to Jesus from heaven as he did at the transfiguration and at Jesus' baptism. But he didn't. He remained silent.

We all have a cross. Ours are not worthy of comparison to the cross of Christ. But we all have that place where we feel pain, abandonment, and despair. What is your cross? And what is the question you most often ask God from that cross?

Sometimes blindness is my cross. Sometimes healing is my question. Other times, depression has been my cross, and "How long?" has been my question. In 2012, I had a breast cancer scare—it was my cross, and my question was "What if?" We all have crosses, and we all have questions. And we all have a God who can answer our questions if he chooses to.

God did not answer Jesus' question. God often does not answer our questions either. What do we do then? Do we just sit around waiting, trying not to be bitter? Well, how did Jesus respond to the silence?

"Father, into your hands I commit my spirit" (Luke 23:46).

Jesus' response to God, even when God was silent, was commitment? May I just say I know many people who have given up or gotten mad when their prayers were unanswered. But Jesus' response was not to give up, but rather to press in even harder. Jesus affirmed his commitment to his Father.

Father is a word that denotes relationship, care, and trust. Jesus could have called him *Yahweh* or *El*, denoting his holiness or majesty. But when he committed his spirit to God's care, Jesus called God "Father"—the Aramaic *Abba*, which is like us saying "daddy." *Abba, into your hands I commit my spirit*. It's an intimate, informal, and very warm name to call one's father. Do you think of God as that familiar and tender? He is your *Abba*, and he hears your prayers, my friend. He is worthy of your trust and commitment.

Earlier, when Jesus cried out, "My God, my God, why have you forsaken me?" he used a different word for God—the Hebrew *El*, which means "Almighty God." Jesus knew it was the almighty nature of God that required justice for sin.

El is a title rather than a personal name. It would be like addressing the queen of England as "Your Majesty." Prince Philip can call her Elizabeth because they are married and have an intimate relationship. But in her position as the queen of the United Kingdom of Great Britain and Northern Ireland she is addressed as "Your Majesty."

Jesus affirmed the almighty, majestic nature of God, and in doing so, he acknowledged the authority of God to remain silent as the best response to his prayer. Jesus respected the authority of *El*, but he entrusted himself into the hands of *Abba*. In doing so, he left another example for us in our pain with our unanswered questions. When we find ourselves on a cross with questions, we appeal to *El*, but we commit our spirit to *Abba*.

Jesus' response to silence and abandonment was to restate his commitment and loyalty to his Father. God's commitment to us is not conditional, and our commitment to him should not have conditions either.

My friend, you can trust God unconditionally. You can commit your questions, your pain, your longings, your confusion, and your very life into God's hands. Jesus committed his spirit into God's hands. He could have committed his spirit to God's heart or God's will. But God's hands are always associated with his authority and care.

Committing ourselves into God's hands means we yield to his authority and honor him with our complete trust. But it also means we trust his care. It was with Christ's hands that God fed the five thousand, washed the disciples' feet, and broke bread at the Last Supper. God touched those with leprosy with the hand of Christ and lifted up the woman caught in adultery with his hands. The hands of Jesus are a picture of his care for us.

If you find yourself on a cross with more questions than answers, don't stop seeking answers. When God doesn't give you an immediate answer, it is so he can grant you something you need more—an intimate connection with your *Abba*.

God's silence was the answer to his son's prayer, and Jesus' response was commitment. If God is answering your prayer with silence, can you choose the same response? In the absence of answers, your faith has the opportunity to grow.

Threads of Truth for Your Blanket of Faith

- You, LORD, hear the desire of the afflicted; you encourage them, and you listen to their cry. (Psalm 10:17)
- The eyes of the LORD are on the righteous, and his ears are attentive to their cry. (Psalm 34:15)
- The Spirit helps us in our weakness; for we do not know how to pray as we ought, but that very Spirit intercedes with sighs too deep for words. And God, who searches the heart, knows what is the mind of the Spirit, because the Spirit intercedes for the saints according to the will of God. (Romans 8:26–27 NRSV)
- "Call to me and I will answer you." (Jeremiah 33:3)
- In the morning, LORD, you hear my voice; in the morning I lay my requests before you and wait expectantly. (Psalm 5:3)

Visit jenniferrothschild.com/threads to download free Scripture cards.

PART 4

God, Do You Care?

Depression had unearthed every dark emotion and fear I had tried to keep under wraps.

I'm tired. I feel like I'm always trying to stifle despair and hopelessness.

I'm stuck in this body, with limitations beyond my ability to manage—and I don't even want to try any more.

I'm broken and frail.

I'm too needy.

Even empathy is painful for me. I can't stop crying for others when I hear how they're hurting. I feel their despair, and it is so heavy. But I, too, am broken. I can't help them, and I cannot fix myself.

And I want to feel God's love and acceptance. I need to know God is OK with me, even if I never rise to the level of my past performance.

Those were some of the fragmented thoughts and feelings I battled during my yearlong journey through depression. My vulnerabilities left me feeling like a tangle of exposed nerves, ushering in a host of insecurities I had never experienced before.

Will Phil get tired of me?

Will God get impatient with my lack of faith?

Do people care about me only when I am easygoing, fun, or encouraging?

What happens if I can't be a first-string Christian anymore? What if I'm permanently benched? Will God or anyone else still care about me? Or is their care for me based on my ability to reciprocate?

I had gone through the deep waters of sorrow and absorbed every bitter drop. Now I felt like a saturated sponge, and I couldn't absorb any more pain. After decades of managing the unrelenting demands of blindness, I no longer had the strength or stamina to keep myself afloat. Everything I had held in for so long was spilling out in a Niagara of depression, and I was drowning in it.

I had devoted much of my life to helping others, but now I had nothing left to give. I felt like I was disappointing those who rely on me to be uncomplicated and strong. But I was weak and unsure of everything, drenched in insecurity and neediness.

This was not what I wanted. I did not want to be a constant trickle of insecurity and fear. I did not want to be saturated and spilling over with hopelessness and despair. I just wanted God to hold me tenderly in his hands. I needed to know he could handle my saturated soul with gentleness. But I was at the end of myself and felt like I no longer merited care from God because I could no longer care for others the way I always had.

I need love and acceptance. I can't take any rejection right now. I'm too vulnerable.

It was the first time I had questioned whether or not God's love and concern for me really were unconditional.

God, do you care?

CHAPTER 14

Compassionate Inactivity

Is it not in mercy then that sorrow is allotted unto us?

Egyptian proverb

I've already introduced you to my husband, Phil, but you may not know he's a professor with a PhD, and I sometimes affectionately call him my own personal Dr. Phil. He is sweet, smart, fun, and quirky, but sometimes I think he could use a session or two with the real Dr. Phil because my Dr. Phil has a few issues. And if he were here right now, he would readily admit without a hint of embarrassment that he does have issues—after all, we all do. Not only do his issues not bother him; I think he might actually be *proud* of them!

Take the issue with the laundry. He is perfectly capable of placing his dirty clothes in the hamper conveniently located in our closet. But does he ever do this simple thing that he is perfectly capable of doing? Nope. More often than not, he drops his dirty clothes *right in front of* the clothes hamper!

Throughout our marriage, I've questioned this aggravating behavior and tried to solve the mystery of it: "Honey, if you can just as easily drop your clothes *into* the basket rather than *in front of* the basket, why won't you?" His response? A goofy smirk. Not quick to give up, I once invited him into the closet with me, where I used exaggerated gestures while standing varying distances from the hamper, all the while counting out loud how many seconds it took to toss laundry *into* the basket rather than in front of it. Of course, I also pointed out that even though I cannot see the basket, I rarely miss! In one really desperate moment, I tried to shame him into compliance: "So, smart guy, you can manage getting a PhD, but you can't manage to get a dirty T-shirt into the laundry basket? *Really?*"

Nada. Zip. Zilch. No reaction except that same goofy smirk! I just can't make the man do something he is capable of doing if he chooses not to. Ugh! The floor of my closet is forever doomed. I know he really doesn't care about his pile of dirty clothes, but when I'm having a bad day, the same laundry I laugh at on most days can make me wonder, "Doesn't he care about *me*? At least enough to drop his clothes in the basket?" Now, I know there are bigger issues in life than laundry. I am just making a big deal of this one funny little issue to make a much more serious point.

And that point is? Drumroll please ... If I get frustrated with an earthly relationship that doesn't meet my expectation of good and right behavior in the little things of life, how much more confused and disappointed am I when my relationship with God falls short of my expectations in the big, very consequential areas of life? When God is capable of doing something in my life—like healing or delivering—but chooses not to, I can feel frustrated and hurt. And when I can't coax God to do what I want, when I can't influence him or pressure him into doing something he is perfectly capable of, I start to wonder if God just doesn't care.

Perhaps you can relate. The circumstances of your life have been disappointing or devastating, and you're wondering why God doesn't do what he is capable of doing. Why did he let it happen? Why didn't he heal when you asked? Why has he seemed distant and uncaring as you suffered? Does God even care?

Is God Caring?

When God doesn't step in and rescue us from the deep hurt and fear of life's tough challenges, it's not unreasonable to wonder, "God, do you even care?" It's a hard question but also an honest one. Whenever I wrestle with a question like this, the best way I know to deal with it is to consider what God says about himself. For example, maybe the reason God seems uncaring at times is because he never claimed to be the kind of God who *does* care about every little thing anyway. And let's face it, to God even our big stuff like cancer, autism, car accidents, hurricanes — you know, the things God could prevent or remedy but doesn't always — maybe to him those are just little things.

So *does* he care? It's one thing to come up with a Sunday school answer to that question, but it's quite another to consider it in the context of real life and real suffering. If we're going to understand what it really means that God is caring when life is difficult, some of our best evidence is found in the real lives and real suffering of men and women in the Bible who wrestled with this question. Specifically, let's consider the stories of two Old Testament guys — Job and Jonah.

Job

Job's story tells us a lot about human suffering and the character of God. Job was considered by all to be an upright man. He was faithful to God, his family, his work, and his community. (And I bet he even threw his dirty clothes in the laundry basket!) Yet, he endured years of heartache and what seemed to be senseless tragedies. He was once wealthy and then lost everything. He was once a proud father of successful and loving children and then lost each one to a terrible storm. His wife disdained him; he lost his health; he experienced terrible depression; and his friends were lousy comforters.

If just one of the devastations Job suffered had occurred in my life, I would have questioned whether or not God was truly caring. After all, God could have preserved Job's wealth and health. He could have protected or rescued Job's children. But despite everything he suffered, Job doesn't accuse God of not caring. Instead, he makes this astonishing statement: "You have granted me life and lovingkindness; and Your care has preserved my spirit" (Job 10:12 NASB). Even though Job's body was covered with sores and his soul covered with questions, he still affirmed God's care for him.

When Job says it was God's *care* that preserved his life, he is referring to God's watchful providence. One use of the Hebrew word translated "care" refers to mustering an army and the meticulous care required to look after those who are enlisted. It denotes vigilance, providence, and custody. It also frequently has the meaning "carefully examine, attend to, take note of, with the implied intention of responding appropriately."* In other words, Job knew that God was fully aware of what was happening to him. Even in the midst of his suffering, he trusted that it was God who preserved him and that he owed his very life to God's constant care.

What an astounding perspective! Job believed that the God who allowed sickness, death, and loss was the same God who cared for him. The God who chose *not* to heal, protect, or prevent calamity was the same God who preserved his life. Although his life was shattered by catastrophic losses, he was convinced it was nevertheless God's care that sustained him. Hold that thought as we consider another eye-opener of God's caring character as revealed in the story of Jonah.

Jonah

If Job was an upright man, the reluctant prophet Jonah was a downright hooligan. God told Jonah to go to the people of Nineveh—one of Israel's fiercest enemies—and call them to turn away from their wickedness. Jonah didn't want to because he didn't want God to give those undeserving scoundrels any mercy. So instead of sailing to Nineveh, Jonah took a boat to Tarshish, which was in precisely the opposite direction. But after enduring a life-threatening storm and being deposited on a beach with the help of a large fish, Jonah finally gave up and went to Nineveh.

---

* Tyler F. Williams, *"pāqad,"* in *New International Dictionary of Old Testament Theology and Exegesis*, Willem A. VanGemeren, ed. (Grand Rapids: Zondervan, 1997), 3:659.

When Jonah preached repentance and told the Ninevites of God's truth and grace, they responded by turning from their terrible ways and humbly drawing near to God. Seeing their repentance, God had compassion on them and "did not bring on them the destruction he had threatened" (Jonah 3:10). This was precisely what Jonah did not want:

> *But to Jonah this seemed very wrong, and he became angry. He prayed to the LORD, "Isn't this what I said, LORD, when I was still at home? That is what I tried to forestall by fleeing to Tarshish. I knew that you are a gracious and compassionate God, slow to anger and abounding in love, a God who relents from sending calamity."*
>
> Jonah 4:1–2

Oh, the irony! Here we have a man who knows that God is gracious and compassionate but wishes he *weren't*! In fact, Jonah was so convinced about God's caring nature that he risked his life in an effort to prevent any of that care from reaching Nineveh. For Jonah, the issue was not whether or not God was caring, but the fact that God's care extended to people he felt didn't deserve it. Jonah could not have cared less, yet his story shows us that God could not have cared more. That is how he is—always compassionate and mindful of us.

Is God Forgetful?

If we accept the testimonies of Job and Jonah—which clearly point to the truth that God does care—we can still wonder about questions like these:

If God is so caring, then why won't he act when he can?
Is it that he doesn't care enough?
Are our issues just at the bottom of the totem pole of heaven?
Does he sometimes just forget to care about what we care about?

The great psalmist Asaph struggled with similar questions and difficult emotions. In the midst of painful circumstances he wrote,

"Has [God's] unfailing love vanished forever? Has his promise failed for all time? Has God forgotten to be merciful? Has he in anger withheld his compassion?" (Psalm 77:8–9). The psalmist was so lost in despair he could not be comforted (Psalm 77:2). His pain intensified into doubts and questions. Had God's loving-kindness simply evaporated or expired? Was God angry and unwilling to be compassionate? Or had he somehow just forgotten to be caring?

My friend, I bet you've felt that way; I sure have. I know it hurts when you feel forgotten in your pain. When deep sorrow or confusion is deeply entrenched in your life, it can seem that God's compassion is conspicuously absent. But it isn't. God will not and cannot forget to be compassionate to you.

No matter how dark your circumstances may be, God wants you to know it is impossible for him to forget you or to neglect caring for you. Here's how we know this to be true. Look at God's promise spoken through the prophet Isaiah, "Can a mother forget the baby at her breast and have no compassion on the child she has borne? Though she may forget, I will not forget you!" (Isaiah 49:15).

It is impossible for a mother to forget her child — no matter whether that baby is twenty-one days old or twenty-one years old. Even if you're not a mom, you had one, right? You know intuitively that motherhood brings with it an urge to love, protect, and nurture. And this caring impulse isn't limited to human mothers — just try to stroke a baby bird or cuddle a bear cub, and you'll soon find yourself at the wrong end of some intense mother love! Moms don't forget, and neither does God.

When our oldest son, Clayton, had emergency surgery as an eight-month-old baby, it was such a scary day for Phil and me. I knew all the risks, and I hated handing over my sweet baby to a surgeon. I felt a deep and unfamiliar sorrow and pain because of my sweet son's pain. I wished it could have been me instead of him. There was no way I could forget my son. I loved him too much and cared for him too much to forget. I was also nursing at the time and had to stop immediately. If you've ever nursed a baby, you know it's definitely not the ideal way to stop. It's extremely painful. Let me just say this, sister—even if I had wanted to forget my baby and forget being compassionate, I could not. My personal pain kept my son's pain front and center. Of course, I chose not to forget my son—and I could not forget, even if I wanted to.

If human moms like me have such deep and instinctual compassion and care, how much more does our heavenly Father remember us and desire to show us his compassion? God doesn't forget to be compassionate; it's just that sometimes his compassion comes in ways that are hard to recognize.

Mysterious Compassion

When we think about our hard or painful circumstances, we may find it hard to understand how God can truly care if he lets them remain. Why doesn't he show his compassion in a way we can recognize? Or maybe a better question is, "Why does he choose to show his compassion in such mysterious ways?" We often assume that God's apparent inactivity in our situation is evidence of his lack of compassion, when really it may be his way of protecting us, providing for us, or preserving us.

Here's what I mean. I've wondered who I would be and where I would be if God had showed his compassion to me by healing me rather than allowing me to remain blind. When I was growing up, I wanted to be an artist, and I had some talent that could have made that dream a reality. But when I lost my sight as a teen, becoming an artist was no longer a possibility. I could have assumed that if God is compassionate, he would have healed me so I could see and realize my dream. But he didn't. Yet, in his mysterious compassion, he positioned me to express my creativity without my eyes. He exposed me to music and writing—creative outlets I might never have explored if I had been able to see.

Would I be a more fulfilled and content person just because I could see? Or, without the protection of blindness, would I have become fiercely independent and potentially isolated from God and others? What if God had not compassionately withheld healing? Would I be absorbed with my looks or social status? Oh, man, I deal with enough pride being blind; I can't imagine what a self-absorbed, full-of-myself gal I might have been if God hadn't compassionately allowed blindness to soften and humble me. If my life had been easier, what would I really have gained compared to how my loss has granted me such opportunity and blessing? Would you even be reading this book if God had showed his care for me by healing me? Sometimes God's compassion hurts, but it is the severe compassion that only a perfect, kind, and loving Father gives.

So what about you? Might God be showing his compassion to you like he did to Job by allowing your pain to remain rather than by removing it? How might your pain or unanswered questions display God's care for you? Ask yourself the following questions:

- Are there any ways in which my pain has been a source of *protection* for me? If so, how?
- In what ways has God used this situation to *provide* for me? What has my pain taught me about God or myself that I couldn't have learned any other way?
- How might God be using my difficulties to *preserve* me? Has my painful circumstance saved me from making destructive choices or taking wrong paths?

I began this chapter by telling you about my quirky husband and his laundry issue, but, really, I must conclude with a confession: I am the one with the issue. You know what my issue is? I've been reluctant to accept my Dr. Phil for who he is in all his messy, absentminded-professor splendor! Instead of trying to control him and get his behavior to make sense to me, I just need to trust his good character and enjoy the many other ways he shows his care for me. And you know, perhaps that's how we need to think about it when we struggle with the question of God's care for us. Maybe you and I just need to accept that *God does care*, and then trust his good character—even when it doesn't make sense to us. The fact that our suffering remains when God has the ability to remove it may be a sign of compassion we don't yet understand. His concern for us outweighs his desire for our comfort.

My friend, you may not *feel* he cares, but that doesn't mean he does not care. He may allow your suffering to remain because he is using that hard thing to protect you from something far worse, preserve you for something far better, or provide for you what you don't even realize you need. His apparent inactivity is not a sign that he is forgetful or lacks compassion, but rather an indication of his deep compassion and higher purpose for you.

If you need to be assured that God cares for you, give him your sorrows, questions, and tears. You will find he is a compassionate God who cares deeply for you. You are invited to "give all your worries and cares to God, for he cares about you" (1 Peter 5:7 NLT). He does care for you and about you. His compassion will not fail you. He will not forget to care for you, my friend. His compassion may be mysterious and even feel severe, but you can trust him. Don't let your "issue" keep you from recognizing and receiving God's compassion.

P.S.: I offer a final goofy smirk of my own as I wonder how Jonah and Asaph handled their laundry? Huh, Phil?!

CHAPTER 15

Where There's Ability, There's Responsibility

Most powerful is he who has himself in his own power.

Seneca, *Moral Letters to Lucilius*

A helpless father leaves the hospital faced with a grieving wife and the task of purchasing a tiny casket. God could have answered their frantic prayers. Why didn't he?

A mother pleads with an anonymous kidnapper via the six o'clock news for the safe return of her ten-year-old daughter. A God who sees all and cares for all can easily pluck her beloved child from that terror. Why doesn't he?

An adolescent son takes on the role of running the household and parenting his two younger siblings because Dad is out of the picture and Mom is lost in a downward spiral of alcoholism. The son begs God to please keep his mom from drinking. Why doesn't he?

You could likely add your own difficult situation to the list—a chronic illness, a devastating loss, a broken relationship, a dark depression, a broken dream. And you've probably asked the question about why a caring God allowed it to happen. *Why, God? Why didn't you do something then? Why don't you do something now?*

One way some people try to make sense of these questions is to think of God's power as constrained. The thinking is that maybe God is compassionate but doesn't step in and clean things up because he's somehow limited. Perhaps he used his power to set the world in motion but then stepped back and just let everything run its course. So he's a compassionate God who would help if he could, but he planned all along to just let us figure things out on our own. That would mean he does care, but he doesn't have the ability to step in because he has granted us free will.

So the real questions become, "Is God capable? Does his power have limits? Or is his power as real as his compassion?" In the last chapter, we discovered how God revealed himself as compassionate through the lives of Job and Jonah. In the life of the prophet Jeremiah, we discover what God reveals about his power.

The prophet Jeremiah lived during the most critical period of the nation of Judah. He saw the destruction of Jerusalem and the temple. He preached, wept, and begged his people to turn away from idols and back to God. But they wouldn't.

So God told Jeremiah to go down to the potter's house and observe a potter molding clay and shaping a pot. While Jeremiah watched, God taught him two truths: (1) God has the ability and authority to create or destroy nations and people, and (2) it is as ridiculous for us to question God's power as it is for a pot to say to the potter, "What are you doing? Why did you make me this way?"

God asked, "Can I not do with you, Israel, as this potter does?... Like clay in the hand of the potter, so are you in my hand, Israel" (Jeremiah 18:6). Through Jeremiah, God states that he can do as he chooses with his people. He has the power and ability to create and re-create, to shape and destroy. God shows his power "as seemed best to him" (Jeremiah 18:4). In other words, God shows his power in the way he chooses.

And it isn't always as we would choose, is it?

God's Power and Authority

God's power is beyond our ability to perceive or grasp. He is omnipotent. That literally means "all-powerful." If we affirm that God is caring and compassionate and that he is powerful beyond bounds, why doesn't he act when we ask? If God has the *ability* to act, shouldn't he also have the *responsibility* to act? Before addressing that question, allow me to share a Phil story that may shed some light on things.

When Phil and I were newlyweds, we lived in a rickety-rackety-shack little apartment in West Palm Beach, Florida. We were smack-dab in the middle of the worst part of town and had our bikes and barbeque grill stolen to prove it. Blaring sirens serenaded us each night as we fell asleep. Although I wasn't fond of this less-than-secure environment, Phil used it as a launchpad for heroics. On several occasions he chased away "bad guys" from our backyard. He did that once while barely clad in a shabby pair of gym shorts. It was bad enough that the police and the public saw him dressed that way, but then who should happen by the crime scene but the vice president of the university where Phil taught! Indeed, he got there just in time to behold my shirtless husband in all his saggy gym-shorts splendor.

The story Phil most loves from his superhero days in Crimeville was the time he saw a guy dart behind our apartment carrying a TV. Faster than a speeding bullet (well, you know), Phil ran outside and began to chase the bad guy. (This time fully dressed, I might add.) Bad guy saw Phil. Bad guy dropped TV. Phil trailed him for blocks until the thief got into a congested part of town. At that point, the bad guy began to walk casually along the sidewalk, blending into the crowd. Phil was concerned the bad guy might have a gun, so he hid behind trees but continued to follow him covertly. The police had been called, and their approaching sirens alerted Phil that help was on the way. As soon as the patrol car pulled up, Phil sprang out from behind a bush and ran toward the villain. He threw himself at the startled man's ankles, hooked them in his arm, and yelled, "Officer, I got him!" It was a proud and powerful Barney Fife moment!

Phil's antics showed off his power but also highlighted the fact that he lacked authority. Power without authority is incomplete. He could have clung to the bad guy's ankles for hours because my man is strong and powerful, but without authority, his power was incapable of securing justice. Because Phil had the ability (and a pretty inflated hero complex), he felt he had the responsibility to act. And he did. One who has the ability to help or rescue should help or rescue. But even though he fulfilled his responsibility as a citizen, it still wasn't enough without a greater authority of law enforcement stepping in to secure justice on behalf of the good people of West Palm Beach.

Power Yields to Authority

Authority trumps power every time. Why? Because one's power is only as great as one's ability to exercise it. Even limitless power can be limited by authority. The choice to refrain from exercising power does not mean one is powerless. It simply means that sometimes one who has power chooses to yield it to greater authority. God possesses both ultimate power and ultimate authority—and our God of compassion often yields his power to his authority.

It's a challenging concept to understand, so maybe a story will help. In the aftermath of the Civil War, an itinerant atheist made his way across the country preaching an anti-God message. He sought to convince his audiences that God simply did not exist. He touted his position and then ended each message with a defiant dare: "If there is a God, then certainly he is powerful enough to strike me dead right now." Only silence followed. The onlookers were hushed, and from heaven there came no response.

The scoffer took the silence of heaven as proof of his argument; therefore God did not exist. Or if God did exist but didn't act, then God must not be powerful. Yet I believe there is another way to interpret the silence—a perspective that disproves the atheist's conclusion and further confirms God's amazing power and compassion. If God had thundered down lightning and hail on the man, doing so certainly would have proved that God had power over the elements. But a far more significant evidence of God's power can be seen in his willingness to withhold his power.

The Bible includes many examples of God revealing himself as powerful, but I especially love what the apostle Paul says in his letter to the Romans. His inspired words help us understand more about why God sometimes chooses not to act when he's asked or challenged.

> *What if God, although choosing to show his wrath and make his power known, bore with great patience the objects of his wrath— prepared for destruction? What if he did this to make the riches of his glory known to the objects of his mercy, whom he prepared in advance for glory—even us, whom he also called, not only from the Jews but also from the Gentiles?*
>
> Romans 9:22–24

Paul is declaring that God endures our sinfulness with patience. He does this to make known the riches of his mercies and forbearance. Instead of exercising his power, God yields his power to his authority. His power then becomes evident not in wrath but in his patience toward us and through his mercy and willingness to forbear.

God Forbears

To understand God's forbearance, we need to step back for a moment and remember that all of us are born with the same human disease—sin. Now, if you don't like that word, bear with me. Admitting you have sin is like admitting the sky is blue. It's just stating a fact. We are all born with the seed of sin in us, and then we willingly water it, feed it, and see the fruit grow in our lives. Some of us are more sanitized sinners than others. We avoid the so-called big sins and specialize in the small stuff of white lies, harboring bad thoughts about others, exceeding the speed limit, and entertaining secret lusts. We tend to think it's only the murderers and extortionists who are the real sinners. But the point is not *how* we sin; the point is that we all do sin.

Many know the familiar truth that "all have sinned and fall short of the glory of God" (Romans 3:23). Put simply, sin is what separates us from God, both in nature and proximity. The result of all sin is death (Romans 6:23). We experience this in our physical bodies—we are born in flesh under the curse of sin, so our bodies die. But the greater result of sin is the separation it creates between us and God. Because we choose sin over God, we should have to pay the full price of our sin, which is death. But we don't have to because Jesus paid it for us. He died the death intended for us and took the penalty for our sin so we wouldn't have to. If we put our faith in what Jesus Christ did for us, we don't have to live separated from God.

What does that mean for you and me? It means God could hold us accountable for our sin, but instead he *forbears*. In describing this truth to his readers, the apostle Paul cautions them not to "show contempt for the riches of [God's] ... forbearance" (Romans 2:4). Other translations of the Bible render *forbearance* as "tolerance" or "patience." The Greek word *anochē* (an-okh-ay), or forbearance, is perhaps best understood with an image rather than a definition. Visualize the hand of God upraised and ready to strike a just blow against the sinner. Just then, the other hand of God rises to stop the blow by grasping his arm and pulling it back. In his restraint, God displays he has power over himself. He chooses not to act, even though he could. He chooses to *forbear*.

What a powerful and kind God! He *could* and *should* hold us accountable for our sins but chooses not to. God cares about you and me so deeply that he chooses to restrain himself.

His forbearance—his willingness to refrain from taking justifiable action—demonstrates a compassion so great that it is nearly beyond our ability to comprehend. And yet this very same forbearance that allows us to escape punishment for sin also allows us to experience suffering. Think about this. The restraint and forbearance God uses when it comes to our sin show his compassion, and as a result we are drawn closer to him. The restraint and forbearance God shows in allowing us to suffer—his kind unwillingness to heal even though he could, and the patience he shows as he allows our heartaches to remain—demonstrate his severe compassion. He is our Father. And he doesn't like to see his children struggle. Can't you imagine how a perfect Father God must long for his children to have all he originally intended us to have? But he forbears in that he allows his greater purpose to prevail. He restrains himself from protecting us from the very things that draw us closer to him and conform us more closely to the image of his Son, Jesus.

God's Compassionate Restraint

Oh, my friend, I know you're trying to trust God and understand his ways. I struggle with the same. I'm fully confident that God cares about me and has the power to heal my blindness, but he doesn't choose to show his care for me in the ways I hope—not yet, anyway. Does that mean he doesn't care? I don't think so. Instead, I think it means he cares enough to allow me to struggle and find a deeper understanding of his purposes for me and a deeper connection to his heart.

I don't really understand all the reasons God shows restraint when he could act. But this I know: he is compassionate and good. So, though your experience of suffering may not *feel* good, it can *bring* good to you. In fact, Scripture gives a couple of really good examples of why God often shows restraint.

1. God sometimes chooses not to act in order to give us time to acknowledge our sin or to seek him. For example, in pronouncing judgment on Israel, God spoke through the prophet Hosea, describing himself as a lion who would "tear [Israel] to pieces" but then "return to my lair until they have borne their guilt and seek my face—in their misery they will earnestly seek me" (Hosea 5:14b, 15).

Suffering itself doesn't make us need God; rather, it exposes the fact that we always have and always will need him. For that reason alone, suffering can be a divinely merciful act because it compels us to embrace our need for God.

How might this idea that suffering exposes our need for God

apply to your painful or confusing circumstances? Has your hard situation allowed you to see the depths of your need for God—not just for the difficulty you face but for everything in life? Has it compelled you to seek God with more intensity? Enabled you to rely more fully on God's forgiveness and grace?

2. God uses his restraint and forbearance to demonstrate his compassion and draw us closer to him. Consider this beautiful description from the prophet Isaiah, "Yet the LORD longs to be gracious to you; therefore he will rise up to show you compassion. For the LORD is a God of justice. Blessed are all who wait for him!" (Isaiah 30:18). Isaiah's words remind us that God wants to be good to us and show us compassion. Yet sometimes he doesn't "rise up" within the timetable we desire. And so we have to draw near, stay close, and wait on him. The Lord does love justice, but because he loves you, sometimes you have to wait for it. Could this be the reason he hasn't stepped in and removed your suffering? Is God perhaps restraining his power on your behalf in order to draw you to a deeper, better place?

Imagine what might happen if you got everything you want from God. How might that change your life? Would it deeply satisfy your soul? Give you lasting peace and contentment? If there's anything I've seen clearly in my blindness, it is this—that true soul contentment and lasting peace aren't achieved when hardships are removed; they only come from a relationship with God.

If you're struggling with discontentment or bitterness, do you really think those character issues would immediately disappear if your suffering did? I wish! But if I am a discontented blind woman, then I would be a discontented sighted woman if God were to heal me. Our character rarely gets better just because our circumstances do. Only a deep, satisfying encounter with God changes our character. Don't settle for less. You are too highly valued and cared for by God to miss out on what he can lovingly accomplish in you through your suffering.

Press in, my friend. Find the purpose of God's compassionate restraint.

If we plead for God's power, then we must accept his authority that comes along with it. His power may be capable of fixing our hard situation, but his authority may not deem it best. It's a dynamic that perhaps parents especially can relate to, because we understand what it means to exercise compassionate restraint with our children.

When Connor was in second grade, he came home one Friday afternoon and said, "Mom, get out your laptop so I can work on Microsoft Word!"

I complied with the seven-year-old Bill Gates and started up Baby Dell. Before continuing with the story, I should tell you I named my laptop. Ask anyone in an airport with me; I always take Baby Dell out of his bag as I go through security and introduce him to the TSA agents, who handle him with care! I'm sure they think I'm a little loony, but no one messes with my computer!

I placed Baby Dell on Connor's lap and heard Connor pecking at the keys. "Mom, don't listen," he said. "I'm writing you a letter."

I assured him I wasn't listening, but it's really hard for a mother to ignore her child and for a blind woman not to hear—especially when Baby Dell talks. (When Baby Dell talks, Mama Jenn listens!)

I heard Connor spelling, "Dear Mom, I l-o- . . ."—he was trying to type "love," but he couldn't find the "v." He paused and grunted.

I silently cheered him on. *Come on, Connor—it's right by the c!* I had the power to help him. I could have stepped in because I also had the ability, but would that have been best for him? After a minute, I heard it: "v" followed by "e," and soon the document was complete. He proudly read it to me, and I cheered.

Though I had the ability to intervene, my Supermom power yielded to my wise and compassionate Supermom authority. I loved Connor so much that I knew if I asserted my power, in the long run it would not be the most compassionate act because he would not have found the "v" on his own. He needed to struggle, search, and persevere in order to learn. You get the hard point I'm making from this simple story. God's restraint really is a merciful reflection of his great compassion for you.

Trusting God's Compassionate Authority

God allows you to struggle, even though his power could prevent it, because his wise and compassionate authority knows that the benefit of your struggle far outweighs the comfort you may experience from his rescue. God allows you to search for answers, even though he has the power to reveal the answers, because his compassionate authority knows you will gain greater revelation than mere answers as you pursue and persevere. He often sits back and watches you try to find the "v" because he loves you so incredibly much.

Will you trust his authority? Will you trust that his choice is best? Will you trust that he is compassionate and cares deeply for you? Will you concede that God may be doing something productive and purposeful in the midst of your pain?

My friend, consider this with me. To embrace the concept of God's compassion and forbearance as it applies to our sins, yet to reject it as it applies to our suffering, is to reject part of the character of God. And if we don't experience God's wholeness, we will never experience our own. My prayer for you is that God will grant you the understanding and grace to plead for God's power and at the same time to accept and trust his authority.

CHAPTER 16

If You Care, Get Me Out of Here

When the train goes through a tunnel and the world gets dark, do you jump out? Of course not. You sit still and trust the engineer to get you through.

Corrie ten Boom

In the spring of my senior year, my high school class went on a two-week, seven-country tour of Europe. Thankfully, our principal required that each student journal every day. If not for my journal, many of the details from that once-in-a-lifetime trip would be forever lost in the recesses of my now forty-something brain. One memory that does stick out, though, even without the aid of my journal, is the day we ventured into the depths of an Austrian salt mine.

We donned white, smocklike hooded garments and were given two instructions: walk single file and don't touch the walls of the mine. I fell in line behind a classmate, Scott, and my friend Stacy was right behind me. The deeper we descended into the cavelike mine, the colder it got. The sounds in the cave were narrow and piercing, and several of my classmates enjoyed hearing their voices echoing back and forth. Everybody was cheerful and noisy on our way down. I chatted with Stacy, who walked directly behind me, but I didn't speak to Scott. In fact, I'm pretty sure Scott and I had never really spoken to each other in the entire four years we'd attended school together. But the deeper we descended into the mine, the closer Scott and I became. And by closer, I mean he was literally an inch away.

The walls of the cave soon became a tunnel that grew progressively narrower. It was hard to avoid brushing against the walls as we continued our descent, and I began to feel anxious. My chest felt as constricted as the tight space around me. My breathing grew shallow. I couldn't stop thinking about how low and narrow the passage was becoming. I felt trapped, and that feeling awakened a "get me out of here" instinct I didn't even know I had! At one point, I tried to turn around and tell Stacy what I was feeling, but the tunnel was so narrow I couldn't even do that. That's when I panicked. I wanted out of that mine—I wanted out of there even if it meant rapture or alien abduction!

That was the day I discovered claustrophobia. I know, I know, you wouldn't think a nearly blind teenager could have that experience, right? But believe me when I tell you that you don't have to see a tight space to know you're in a tight space. The air feels different, more compressed, and sounds are pressed together more tightly. I felt like the air was choking me and there was no escape from the cave or my terror.

I wish I could reconstruct precisely what happened next, but I didn't record the details in my journal. Evidently, that traumatic memory remains deeply buried somewhere in the Austrian mine. I don't know if Scott heard me hyperventilating and praying or if I actually asked for help, but I do know I somehow ended up on his back. For the remainder of our harrowing journey through the mine, Scott carried me piggyback. I buried my face in his neck, but I have no memory that I spoke to him. All I remember is feeling a crazy mix of humiliation and gratitude.

When we at last approached the opening of the mine on the other side, I felt the space widen, the air expand, and the sun fall like a warm blanket. I quickly lifted my face from Scott's jacket, hopped off his back, and muttered a quick thank you. I'm pretty sure that one expression of gratitude was the only conversation we ever had. We never spoke of the incident. In fact, we've never spoken since!

Longing for Deliverance

We all need a rescue from time to time. In fact, you may need one right now, and that's why you've picked up this book. You may be desperate to be delivered from your hard circumstance. Or you may be desperate to be delivered from the sorrow, hopelessness, or depression that came with it. I know how you feel. There have been times I am so sick of being blind that I cry out to God to heal me. And there are even more times when I cry out to God to deliver me from my deep frustration or despair, because sometimes that feels even more debilitating than my blindness. My friend Mandisa captured this kind of desperation perfectly in her song "My Deliverer."

> *I was so helpless, where did the light go?*
> *I had no hope left deep down in my soul.*
> *I was watchin', I was waitin', I was prayin'.*

Could you sing those lyrics along with her with conviction? We've all felt that way before—that we want God to pull us out of our darkness and bring us safely into the light again. The book of Psalms includes many such prayers asking God for deliverance:

- In your righteousness, rescue me and deliver me. (Psalm 71:2)
- Oh, guard my soul, and deliver me! (Psalm 25:20 ESV)
- Be pleased, O Lord, to deliver me! O Lord, make haste to help me! (Psalm 40:13 ESV)
- But you, Sovereign Lord, help me for your name's sake; out of the goodness of your love, deliver me. (Psalm 109:21)

The psalmists appealed to God for deliverance because they knew of his great power and compassion. But they also felt confident in asking for deliverance because God himself had made a promise: "Call on me in the day of trouble; I will deliver you, and you will honor me" (Psalm 50:15). That seems pretty straightforward: *You call; I deliver.* Easy, right? So why doesn't it work like that? If what God says is true, why do we find ourselves in dark places, feeling helpless and longing for deliverance? If God does care and if he has the power to do something about it, why doesn't he deliver us like he promised? Or does he?

Regina's Deliverance

Travel with me back in time to my freshman year at Palm Beach Atlantic University. It was 1982, so get out your banana clip and shoulder pads! I want to tell you a story that may help us understand how God keeps his promise to deliver us. One of my sweetest friends my freshman year was a girl named Regina, a vivacious redhead who truly was always smiling. Of course, I couldn't see her smile, but I could hear it in her voice. No matter what the situation, she always found a reason to smile. For example, the night we left the fair and spent two and a half hours wandering the parking lot in the wee hours of the night trying to find her parked car, she never showed frustration or impatience (unlike me, who had a hefty dose of both those qualities). She just kept grinning and giggling! When we finally found her car, it was because the parking lot was practically empty, not because Regina had a working inner GPS. I learned patience from her. And I learned to let people not only see me smile but also *feel* me smile—because I could always feel her smile. She was warm and kind, and it was so clear that she really loved God and people.

At the end of the first semester, all of us packed our suitcases and headed home for the holiday break. One of Regina's favorite things to do at home was to ride her bike in a nearby park. When she failed to return from one of her rides, her family called the police. Tragically, she had been attacked, raped, and strangled. Her unclothed body was hidden in brush and discovered the following day.

All her friends were shaken and devastated. This wasn't some fictional character on a TV crime show—it was Regina, our dear, sweet friend. If God would let something like this happen to Regina, did he really care about anyone? She loved God, so why didn't he deliver her? Wasn't that his promise?

I remember sitting in the living room with my dad after I heard the news. I couldn't hold back tears as I described what Regina endured. More than once I looked at my dad and asked, "How could God let her go through that?"

"She didn't go through it," my dad said quietly in his gentle Southern drawl. His statement startled me.

"She went *from* it," he said.

I must have looked confused because he went on to explain how God delivers us in different ways. Sometimes he protects us from awful things so we never have to endure them. Other times God delivers us by rescuing us or healing us. Sometimes God brings us through hard things—that's also a form of God's deliverance. But then there are the times that God, out of his great care for his children, delivers us *out of* the horror and *into* glory.

God compassionately took Regina out of her tragedy and into his presence. She was delivered from it—out of it—and into glory, where there are no tears, no crying, and no pain, and the only scars are the ones on the hands of Jesus. That understanding of God's deliverance was and still is such a consolation to my heart. God does keep his promise to deliver, but sometimes God's deliverance doesn't show up in the way we expect it.

Three Kinds of Deliverance

Regina's story is one of great sorrow, yet I still consider it a story of God's deliverance. I don't want to simplify something that is so incredibly wrong and painful by throwing a happy Christian bumper sticker over it. The fact is, sometimes the way God keeps his promises is painful for us. But his ways of deliverance are time-tested by people who have gone before us, and maybe a few of their stories will help to clarify and bring comfort. These folks who walked through the pages of the Bible know God's deliverance. Maybe you will see Regina's story in their stories; or better yet, maybe you will see your own.

God delivered King Hezekiah from *his sickbed* (Isaiah 38).

King Hezekiah was a very sick man and was wasting away on his deathbed. He cried out to God for deliverance and healing. God healed. Hezekiah was delivered *from* his illness through healing.

God delivered the three Hebrew young men through *the fire* (Daniel 3:16–28). Shadrach, Meshach, and Abednego were thrown into a furnace of raging fire because they refused to bow down and worship King Nebuchadnezzar. Their punishment was death by fiery furnace. But witnesses saw a miraculous sight—not only were the men not burned; they were walking around in the fire! And then there appeared a fourth man among them, whom onlookers described as a "son of the gods." Those brave men came out of the fire without even the smell of smoke on their garments. They were delivered *through* the fire.

God delivered Stephen out of *his stoning and* into *heaven* (Acts 7:54–60). The good news of Jesus Christ was stirring up some bad blood among Jewish religious leaders. Stephen was caught in the conflict, falsely accused of heresy, and ultimately dragged outside the city to be stoned by a mob. As he was pelted by stones, Stephen asked Christ to receive his spirit. He died as a result of a horrific stoning. God took him *out of* that terror and *into* his presence.

Sometimes we don't feel the impact of Bible stories because they happened such a long time ago. So let me show you exactly what I mean by sharing the stories of three people who are in my life. Each of the three experienced God's deliverance when it came to cancer.

God delivered my dad from *cancer*—he healed him in 2010. God used the hands of a surgeon but beyond a doctor's ability, God put his healing hand on my dad and removed any trace of the disease, much to the doctor's amazement. Just like he did for King Hezekiah, God delivered him *from* the cancer.

God is delivering my friend Rob through *cancer*. Rob still has the disease, is in treatment, and has diligently prayed for healing. God has not chosen to heal him yet. It has been more than ten years since he was first diagnosed, and during the past decade, Rob has been a light of hope to all he meets. God is delivering Rob *through* cancer, like he delivered the three Hebrew men *through* the fire.

Most painful to me is the story of my friend Genia. *God delivered Genia* out of *cancer and* into *heaven.* She was about ten years older than me and was both a mentor and confidante. She was deeply loved by those in her church and community, and everyone prayed diligently and in faith that God would deliver her from this cruel disease. I really thought he would because Genia was so full of faith and such a blessing to so many. But he didn't. After a long, hard fight, God delivered Genia *out of* cancer and *into* heaven on June 6, 2012. God delivered her the same way he delivered Stephen—*out of* the trial and *into* glory!

When you consider the different ways God keeps his promise to deliver us, can you see his deliverance in your circumstance? Has he delivered you *from* something? Has he delivered you *through* something? Do you see how he may deliver you *out of* it and *into* a better place?

Based on the many ways the Bible describes God's deliverance, I believe God also delivered Regina. It wasn't in the way I would have chosen, yet I believe it was his compassionate choice.

God Will Deliver You

Perhaps you have endured something so awful that you are weeping right now just thinking about it and wondering why God let it happen. Maybe the fact you're reading this right now is an indication that God is still in the process of delivering you. He is delivering you *through* it for a purpose higher than living in bitterness or fear. He is delivering you through it because he cares deeply for you. But his compassion really does come in tough packages sometimes. I wish I knew all the answers. The one thing I do know is this: God *does* deliver, and when we can't understand his methods, we must choose to trust his character.

In the salt mines so many years ago, my classmate Scott may not have fully grasped how heroic and compassionate it was for him to carry me out of that dark place. I was desperate to be rescued from the mine that day, and he was my rescuer. He didn't rescue me *from* it, but his quiet responsiveness rescued me *through* it. I didn't know Scott well, but I knew one thing—he cared enough to literally carry me! Because God cares for us, that's what he does for us—he carries us.

God will deliver you because he is your deliverer. He sometimes allows you to remain in the darkness, reminded of your frailty. Sometimes he doesn't deliver you from your heartache in the timetable and way you would choose. But he does and will always deliver you through it. And eventually, he will carry all of us to the place where the sun is forever radiant and warm, to the place where we will forever express our gratitude for all the ways he loves us.

If you are longing to be delivered from a tough situation, let God carry you through every twist and turn until he takes you home.

CHAPTER 17

Spectator Grace

All God's blessings go together, like links in a golden chain. If he gives converting grace, he will also give comforting grace.

C. H. Spurgeon, *Morning and Evening*

A smartly dressed woman confidently paced the stage while explaining stress management to an audience of business professionals. The entire time she spoke, she held a glass of water in her hand like the Statue of Liberty holds up her torch. She continued to speak without even acknowledging the glass of water. Everyone in the audience expected her to eventually ask them, "Half empty or half full?" and explain the importance of a positive attitude. But that's not what she did. The question she finally asked was this, "How heavy is this glass of water?" The answers the audience gave ranged from eight ounces to twenty ounces.

"How much this water weighs doesn't actually matter," she said. "What matters is how long I hold it. If I carry it for a minute, that's not a problem. No matter how heavy it is, I can handle it. If I hold it for an hour, my arm will start to ache. If I hold it for a day, you will have to call an ambulance! In each case, it's the same weight; but the longer I hold it, the heavier it feels." She paused a moment to let the illustration sink in. "And that's the way it is with burdens and stress. If we carry our burdens all the time, sooner or later, the burden will feel heavier and heavier. We won't be able to carry on."

Carrying a burden is one thing; carrying a burden for a very long time is another. Like the glass of water, even a relatively small hardship can wear us down the longer we carry it. And when we are also carrying the weight of someone else's burden along with our own, it can feel like a supersized glass of solid lead. When a loved one carries a heavy burden day in and day out, we feel the weight of it right along with them. When they are struggling, we struggle too.

When we're struggling with long-term burdens that show no signs of changing, we can take comfort in knowing that God's compassion and grace also show no signs of changing. *Charis* (khar-ece) is the Greek word used throughout the New Testament that we translate as "grace." In secular usage, *charis* would have been used to describe a fine wine or a poetic way of speaking. People were said to possess *charis* when they were gracious or artful. One could win the *charis* favor of another by having *charis*—charisma!

Charis also had ethical implications. For example, it was used to express the notion of give and take, or reciprocity, between individuals and community members. Even in its ancient secular use, *charis* suggests benevolence that shows favor and kindness to someone of a lower rank or class. *Charis*, grace, is compassionate. So when your heart is heavy with burdens, the question of whether or not God cares is answered with one word—grace.

Is Grace Enough?

New Testament writers drew on this larger cultural understanding of *charis* to form our biblical understanding of grace. The apostle Paul shows this in his second letter to the church in Corinth. He wrote, "You know the grace [*charis*] of our Lord Jesus Christ, that though he was rich, yet for your sake he became poor, so that you through his poverty might become rich" (2 Corinthians 8:9). Do you see the give and take in that verse? It is a perfect example of lopsided reciprocity that is beautiful and pleasant for you and me. You can see how favor, generosity, loveliness, and kindness all form the tapestry that communicates grace.

Today we typically describe biblical grace as free and unmerited favor. It is undeserved kindness. Grace is the compassionate gift God gives that carries us from our sin, through our sorrow, and into heaven someday. Through God's grace, he gives us a wealth of resources to bear any burden he allows. Therefore, if God doesn't empty our cup of suffering or take it from us, he will give ample grace (favor, kindness, ability) to bear it. Grace is evidence of God's compassion toward us. It is a complete expression that God does care.

Paul wrote to the church at Corinth that God's grace is "sufficient" (2 Corinthians 12:9). That means it is complete and enough. If every need we have is met in God's grace, why are our burdens still so heavy at times? If God's grace is really enough, why does it sometimes feel so inadequate? Why is the glass still so heavy? Is it God's grace that is insufficient, or is it our understanding of his grace that is insufficient?

Two Kinds of Grace

Over the years, I've been interviewed many times about my journey into blindness. After one particularly interesting magazine interview, I phoned my mom.

"Mom, I just finished an interview, and I really think the writer is going to do a good job. I think you'll like the article. And she asked if she could interview you. She said she only has a few questions. Would you be willing to talk to her?"

My mom hesitated before responding. "Honey, I just can't. It's too hard. To that writer, your blindness is a story. To me, your blindness is a wound that still hurts." At the time my mom spoke those painful words, I had been blind for almost thirty years. But it still hurt her because it's hard to watch someone you love carry a burden.

Perhaps you know exactly how she felt because someone in your life is carrying a burden you wish you could fix or pray away. That weight is so heavy, isn't it? As a mom, I know I would much rather bear a hardship for my children than let them suffer through it. It hurts much more to watch them struggle than it does to struggle myself. Is God's grace really sufficient when you feel the weight of such a heavy burden for someone you love?

Consider this—I was fifteen in 1979 when I was diagnosed with retinitis pigmentosa. I was declared legally blind and given the prognosis of total blindness. As I write this book, I am about to turn fifty. I have now lived longer in darkness than I ever did in light. Blindness is still hard. It always will be, but I am used to it. It is my "normal." Because I was granted the burden of blindness, I was also granted the grace (the extra measure of God's favor) to carry it. And God's grace has been sufficient. It has been enough to bear this burden.

I like to describe the grace God gives me as "participant grace." Now, don't go look that up in the Bible because you won't find it. But I think if Paul could read my story, he might just revise his second letter to the Corinthians to include it! But I digress.

I define participant grace as the grace God gives to the one who has to participate in suffering or carry a burden. The child you love who struggles with a special need has participant grace. The elderly parent in hospice care has participant grace. The friend who is fighting cancer has participant grace. It's the sufficient grace God gives to each of us when we carry a difficult burden.

Someone like my mom—and like you if you love someone who is struggling—doesn't have participant grace. Instead, she has what I call "spectator grace," which is the grace God gives to those who watch, love, and pray for others who are burdened. It is just enough grace to come alongside. But it feels very different from participant grace.

If you are a recipient of God's spectator grace and aren't quite sure it is sufficient, may I be a voice of encouragement to you? The burden you feel for your loved one is likely far heavier than the burden your loved one actually carries. God's grace is sufficient for me to be blind. I know grace and I feel grace for my burden because I am the participant. If your loved one has trusted Christ, then he or she has also been granted the grace to bear their heavy burden. Trust that truth for the one you love. Guard yourself from sinking into despair or fear because you just can't imagine how your loved one will make it. You can't imagine how they will make it because your imagination is limited by your experience. You don't experience the same grace that is available to them. They will make it because of participant grace.

You, my dear friend, have spectator grace, which is the grace to watch and come alongside. What you feel for that loved one is in some ways more intense than what they feel for themselves because God's participant grace absorbs some of the sting. It's as if he wraps his arm and his strong right hand around them as they carry their full cup of sorrow each day. That is precisely the image we get when God speaks through the prophet Isaiah: "Do not fear, for I am with you; do not be dismayed, for I am your God. I will strengthen you and help you; I will uphold you with my righteous right hand" (Isaiah 41:10).

If you are a parent, friend, or loved one of a person who is struggling, it's easy to become discouraged and wonder if God cares. You can be overwhelmed by despair or heartache. But don't project the heartache or despair you feel for your loved one onto him or her. In other words, don't imagine that they suffer in the ways you suffer on their behalf. Rest in the sufficiency of God's grace. It is sufficient for spectator suffering. And it is the promise of Scripture: "God is able to make all grace abound to you, so that having all sufficiency in all things at all times, you may abound in every good work (2 Corinthians 9:8 ESV).

Part of the reason I'm convinced of God's deep care for us is because he chose to both participate in our suffering and to "spectate" our suffering. As a loving Father, it must be harder for him to watch us suffer than it is for him to bear our suffering for us. He knows how it feels to bear a heavy burden and how it feels to watch those whom he deeply loves bear heavy burdens. So if he chooses to let us walk with the heaviness, either as spectators or participants, I have to believe it is out of his great compassion for us.

Grace You Can Depend On

My friend, don't depend on your ability to understand the hows and whys of God's compassion; just depend on his grace in your life. This is what Paul describes when he writes, "We have depended on God's grace, not on our own human wisdom" (2 Corinthians 1:12 NLT).

You may feel that the grace you have, whether it is participant or spectator, is just not enough. You still feel such a heavy burden. And yet we have this promise from Scripture: "To each one of us grace has been given as Christ apportioned it" (Ephesians 4:7). The grace you have is the grace you need. God didn't give more to someone else and shortchange you. He gives each of us what we need. So rather than dwelling on your own insufficiency, dwell on his sufficient grace. Your skill, energy, mind-set, or ability may not be enough. That's OK. God's grace is sufficient. My friend, ask God to carry you as you carry your burden. Ask God to hold you up as you hold up another. In your weakness, his strength will be made perfect. You will never know how sufficient his grace is if you don't tap into it.

I like to imagine the smartly dressed stress management trainer tripping off the stage and the whole glass of water splashing onto the floor! And here's why I like that picture. When we carry a burden alone for a long time, we will eventually trip and fall. We will drop the ball, run out of steam, or somehow come face-to-face with the reality that our strength is just not sufficient. When that happens, the burden we carried alone falls onto those who are waiting to help us carry it. God is waiting to help you carry your burden. Accept his invitation: "Cast all your anxiety on him because he cares for you" (1 Peter 5:7). Let your burden fall into a million pieces so God and others can carry it with you and for you.

CHAPTER 18

You Will Be OK

Because of the Lord's *great love we are not consumed, for his compassions never fail.*

Lamentations 3:22

I was stunned. This was not the news I was expecting.

"You have atypical ductal hyperplasia, or ADH," the doctor said. He went on to explain that ADH is an abnormal growth of cells within the breast ducts, which is associated with an increased risk of breast cancer.

My ADH was first discovered during my annual mammogram in November of that year and confirmed by another mammogram in early December. I then had to have a needle biopsy in both breasts a week before Christmas. After the biopsy, the surgeon called and explained the results to Phil and me. Based on the biopsy, he recommended scheduling a lumpectomy in early January.

My first thought was, *Seriously? I'm blind, for heaven's sake! Haven't I already met my quota for suffering?* Well, that was my first thought, and it was quickly followed by an endless stream of the "what ifs." You know—*What if it's cancer? What if they don't get it all? What if I need radiation? What if this is only the beginning of something far worse?* While my mind was racing, evidently Phil's PhD mind was calculating my odds of recovery. "It will be OK," he said with quiet confidence.

It didn't feel OK to me, though—that's for sure. And maybe the reason was that we really didn't *know* it would be OK. None of us really know if it will be OK, do we? Life is uncertain. We all want to live out a story that makes sense. We want poems to rhyme, puzzles to be solved, and weather predictions to be accurate. We just want everything to be OK, and so we manufacture some form of certainty to banish the anxiety of uncertainty. But the truth is, we really don't know whether or not it will be OK. However, it's important to note that the opposite of uncertainty is not certainty; the opposite of uncertainty is openness—openness to God's purposes, God's compassion, and God's plans.

After the call with the surgeon, Phil and I sat in silence for several minutes. My soul was churning, processing. When all the pieces hadn't fallen into place as I wished they had, a tidal wave of fear washed over me. But instead of being a wave of emotion that drowned me, it cleared my head and awakened me to a vital truth I needed to remember: *It* may not be OK, but *I* will be OK.

I had a deep, inner knowing that within the uncertainty I was facing, I could be certain. I knew that no matter what, I would be OK. I knew God cared for me and I was leaning hard into it.

I had the lumpectomy, and the surgery went well. Afterward, I was sore, but Phil was such an attentive caregiver, I eventually felt like myself again—just a little lighter and slightly achy. Thanks to the two golf-ball-sized lumps the doc removed, I am now a 34 used-to-B! And this may be TMI, but I was only tennis balls to begin with. (Gasp! Sorry, Dad.)

A few days after surgery, Phil and I met with the surgeon to hear the results of the pathology tests. All benign! Thankfully, that chapter of my story had an ending that was genuinely OK. However, during the uncertainty, my emotions vacillated between fear and dread, peace and panic. Yet, my soul remained OK even though *it*—my situation—wasn't. Why? Well, it wasn't because of my great faith! I did trust God, but I was scared too. It was because of the Lord's great love, I was not consumed; his compassions never failed (Lamentations 3:22).

The Hebrew word for "compassions" is *rachamim* (ra-kha-meem). The word comes from the root *rechem* (rekh-em), which literally means "womb." What comes to mind when you think of that image? And how do we find an image of compassion there? For starters, a woman's womb is the place where she grows, nurtures, carries, protects, and, at the perfect time, delivers a baby.

The womb serves a distinct purpose for a given amount of time. Perhaps you know of women who had to have labor induced when a pregnancy lasted too long. Our first son was one of those babies. We had to beg, prod, and push Clayton to join us. Oddly enough, he is still that way—on his own schedule! (Too bad a Pitocin drip doesn't work on college students.) Doctors grow concerned when a baby is overdue because remaining in the womb too long can end up hurting both the child and the mother.

Now, think about all of this in the context of God's compassion. The reason you will be OK even if *it* isn't OK is because God will grow you, nurture you, carry you, and at the right time deliver you to the next place. He never stops caring just because he carries you through a tough time. Even in the midst of your heartache or suffering, you are still cradled in his compassion. You are as cared for and protected as a baby in a mother's womb.

What may feel like overwhelming sorrow or trauma is nevertheless within God's compassionate plan. He is not premature in what he allows. His compassions never fail. When you understand that image of God's compassion, you can rest there. You can know that you are cradled within God's perfect care for you. That is why *you* will be OK, my friend—no matter what.

When we trust the compassion of God, we are not consumed by our problems or by fear. Because of his love and compassion, we are not overwhelmed.

I was grateful to be among the 70 percent of women who emerge from lumpectomy surgery with a cancer-free result. Many women receive far more difficult news. I couldn't imagine having endured a series of biopsies and surgery just to find myself facing more surgery or radiation, like many women do. Oh, how my heart goes out to them!

You may be one of those women. You may know and love one.

Do God's compassions fail if the diagnosis isn't good? Is a bad diagnosis evidence of God's failure to be compassionate? A surgery may fail, but God's compassions will not. A treatment may fail, but God's compassions will not. A relationship may fail, but God's compassions will not. A dream may fail, but God's compassions will not.

Have you ever sent an e-mail to a friend or acquaintance and instead of receiving a response, you get a failure notice? I hate those! Mine is very cordial, though. It says something like, "I am sorry. This is a final notice." The point of a failure notice is to inform you that your message got nowhere. It didn't reach the one you intended. It ended in a big failure.

When God sends his compassions to you, there is never a failure notice. Never. He won't run out of compassion. He won't reserve compassion for the biggies in your life and give you nothing in between. His compassions will not fail. So do not fail to expect them. You will not be consumed by fear when you are consumed by the truth that God cares.

God's compassions do not and will never fail. His compassion is ultimately expressed in Jesus Christ. One day, because of Christ, God will wipe away each one of your tears. "For the Lamb at the center of the throne will be their shepherd; he will lead them to springs of living water. And God will wipe away every tear from their eyes" (Revelation 7:17).

If your sorrow seems to disorient you, God's compassions will not fail. He will be your shepherd. If your soul is parched and your spirit thirsty, he will lead you to living water. His compassions will not fail. If your cheeks are streaked with tears because you just don't know if it will ever be OK again, his compassions will not fail you. He will wipe away every tear.

God deeply cares for you, and because he does, even if *it* isn't OK, *you* will be OK.

Threads of Truth for Your Blanket of Faith

- The LORD is good, a refuge in times of trouble. He cares for those who trust in him. (Nahum 1:7)
- The LORD your God is a merciful God; he will not abandon or destroy you or forget the covenant with your ancestors, which he confirmed to them by oath. (Deuteronomy 4:31)
- The LORD's lovingkindnesses indeed never cease, for His compassions never fail. (Lamentations 3:22 NASB)
- As a father has compassion on his children, so the LORD has compassion on those who fear him. (Psalm 103:13)
- The LORD is good and his love endures forever. (Psalm 100:5)

Visit jenniferrothschild.com/threads to download free Scripture cards.

God, Are You Aware?

Being blind is a little like having cancer because it never goes away and no one can truly enter into it with you."

That's what my friend Genia said. She was nearing the end of another round of chemo treatments for cervical cancer, and I was just beginning my yearlong journey through depression. The only thing I could think of to say to her was, "What you're going through is so hard—it's just messy and hard."

"You understand," she said.

But I didn't really. Blindness doesn't take your life. Blindness doesn't zap your energy and make your hair fall out. Blindness doesn't shake you to the bottom of yourself. Blindness doesn't attack your body, stealing your health and your peace.

"It never goes away," she said. "I don't know if I will beat cancer or if cancer will beat me. I really relate to that line from the Psalms: 'Oh, that I had the wings of a dove! I would fly away and be at rest.'"

I did know exactly how that felt—to long for the hope of escape. But you don't escape cancer. You don't escape blindness. You endure them. And you endure the isolation they create, because no one else can truly enter into the soundless, barren place they carve into your soul.

Over the years, people had empathized, prayed, and cried with me; they had cheered me and had done their very best to come alongside me in my blindness. But they just couldn't truly enter into it with me, which only exacerbated the isolation. Even encouragement, which is meant to build a bridge of kindness, too often instead accentuated the chasm of distance between us. After cheery words escaped their lips, the encouragers escaped my darkness and returned to their sighted lives. However sincere their encouragement may have been, it wasn't a pathway to intimacy, but just a glaring reminder that they really didn't know; they couldn't be truly aware of my degree of darkness.

I was aware of all this as I was talking with Genia. I didn't know what it was like to have cancer, so I couldn't enter into it with her fully. But I did understand what it's like to live with a hardship that just won't go away, no matter how much you wish, pray, and hope it will. *That* I understood. And maybe the hard, messy darkness of blindness allowed me to understand just a tiny bit some of her feelings about cancer. So on that stepping-stone of true identification, I entered into cancer with Genia as best I could.

My deepest prayer was that she and I would have less in common in the months to come because she would be cancer free. I prayed her tumor would continue to shrink and her cancer would be healed. I prayed I would walk into her home with cheers of celebration for her recovery, even as I held my white cane for guidance.

Two years later, Genia's battle with cancer ended, but not in the way any of us had hoped. Instead of walking into her home for a celebration, I used my cane to walk into the church for her funeral. Cancer ended. Blindness remained.

But the truth Genia expressed remained with me too.

When something in my life hurts, it can feel like I am utterly alone and nobody really knows what it feels like. It feels impossible for anyone else to really enter in—to see, to understand, to be fully aware of what I'm going through.

Most notably, God. Does he really know? Does he understand? Is he paying attention?

God, are you aware?

CHAPTER 19

God Only Knows

For however devoted you are to [God], you may be sure that he is immeasurably more devoted to you.

Meister Eckhart

At this point in the book, it's time for the first (and only) install-ment of ... wait for it, wait for it ...

"Stump the Reader!"

Welcome! You are the first (and only) contestant.

Here's your first (and only) challenge: Determine what the fol-lowing people or characters have in common:

- Louis Armstrong
- Maxwell Q. Klinger from *M*A*S*H*
- Lena Horne
- Mahalia Jackson
- Zazu from *The Lion King*
- E*Trade baby from the TV commercials

Want the answer? It's OK. You are the only contestant, so either way, you win.

Each of the people or characters listed above has sung some version of the old spiritual "Nobody Knows the Trouble I've Seen." I know, you would have guessed it if given more time! Let me refresh your memory with the lyrics:

Nobody knows the trouble I've seen.
Nobody knows but Jesus.
Nobody knows the trouble I've seen.
Glory hallelujah!

Have you heard it? I remember singing it as a teenager in choir. We don't exactly know when it was written or by whom. The exact origins of spirituals are pretty fuzzy, but we do know these were songs sung by American slaves in the eighteenth and nineteenth centuries as they prayed and waited for freedom. The lyrics expressed their deep longings and sorrows.

What began in the heart of a slave who felt insignificant, unknown, and forgotten has continued through the decades and become a song many people still sing today. Why do you think that is? After all, the song is likely at least two hundred years old. Maybe it's because, though the song is dated, the sentiment it expresses is as real as the sun in the sky above—as current as your own heartbreak and questions.

I met a woman named Jenny who has lived out the unsung questions woven into those lyrics. When she was diagnosed with rheumatoid arthritis as a young woman, she had no idea her life would be forever altered. As a wife and mom now in her forties, she stated, "Sometimes I wonder if God even remembers I still suffer with this. I can't forget. I know it every single day, but does he?"

Jenny's question cuts right to the heart of those lyrics, doesn't it? Every heart has sung some version of "Nobody Knows the Trouble I've Seen." And when we sing those words, we can't help but wonder, "Does that include God? Does he know the trouble I've seen? Is he aware?" I wonder if in the mind of the man or woman who first sang that haunting song was the unsung sentiment, "God *doesn't* know the trouble I've seen."

Does God Really Know?

Does "nobody" include God? Do you ever wonder if God really *does* know what is going on in your world? Does he know what is going on in the whole world? Most people believe that if there is a God (and of course, that's what I believe), then he must know everything. He has to have full awareness or he wouldn't be supernatural, right? Or is that right? Is that what God says about himself?

Let's first establish whether God claims to know everything, to have perfect knowledge, and then we'll consider if and how that may impact us.

The teaching of Scripture is that God knows "every bird in the mountains" and that "the insects in the fields" belong to him (Psalm 50:11). The psalmist states that God "determines the number of the stars and calls them each by name" (Psalm 147:4). Jesus himself said, "Not one of [the sparrows] will fall to the ground outside your Father's care. And even the very hairs of your head are all numbered" (Matthew 10:29–30). The stars God numbers are finite, yet his knowledge is infinite—it cannot be inventoried. He knows every sparrow that falls. He is aware of the very hairs on your head, and he knows every bird in the mountains—and the birds in cages too. He knows the insects in the field and even your pet gerbil.

Sure, the psalmists were using poetic language, and Jesus was perhaps using extreme examples to make his point, but the truth both the psalmists and Jesus communicate about God is clear: God knows all because his knowledge is innate—it's who he is. As an infinite being, God possesses infinite knowledge. This is why we say that God is *omniscient*.

The word *omniscient* means "all-knowing." The word itself has its roots in two Latin words—*omni*, which means "all," and *scient*, which means "knowledge." God's knowledge is ultimate and absolute. God has perfect awareness of everything—stars and sparrows; hairs and hurricanes; a slave in a cotton field and a woman with rheumatoid arthritis in Missouri; our past, present, and future—all is known to God.

The prophet Isaiah described God's knowledge this way: "Who can fathom the Spirit of the LORD, or instruct the LORD as his counselor? Whom did the LORD consult to enlighten him, and who taught him the right way?" (Isaiah 40:13–14). In other words, God is knowledge itself, the ultimate "Knower." There is no one who taught God or who knows more than God.

To put it simply, God claims to possess ultimate and perfect knowledge. But the complexity of that supposedly simple truth for me is that it didn't free the slaves or remove Jenny's arthritis. God's knowledge is perfect, but how do we reconcile the fact that God knows everything with the fact that he still doesn't always do something about it?

Well, that is a question for "Stump the Author"—and it's not the first or only! I would give you an easy answer if there were one. But here is the true answer: God's knowledge is perfect, but our world is not. You may think that statement is the beginning of a discussion on God's omniscience, but for me, it kind of sums it up. Here's why. Our lives and our world are far from perfect. The reason God's knowledge can be perfect yet our lives less than perfect is that God is perfectly good. Huh?

Perfectly Good, Perfectly Personal

Volumes have been written on what I'm about to summarize in a few paragraphs. So please know there is no way I can exhaustively explore and explain this concept. (As if I exhaustively understand it myself!) But in the briefest way, let me try to put plain words around what I mean.

- The goodness of God allows for free will. In God's morally pure and benevolent virtue, he lovingly created human beings and angels with the ability to choose to obey or disobey him.
- Free will allows human beings to choose evil. Our free will is a gift we often abuse, despite its intended purpose for good.
- The human ability to choose evil allows for the consequence of evil.
- The consequence of evil is not only the due suffering of the individual who commits evil but also undue suffering of the innocent.

Whew!

I don't pretend to understand God's ways, but I do trust his heart. God knows all, and God loves all. Because he is loving, God allows freedom to all his creatures. God's allowance of freedom to all means he knows all things—he knows we will blow it, regret it, and suffer the consequences for it. Yet, he still allows us to choose, and he makes all things work together for our eventual good.

Now, if you can accept that God is omniscient and good, does that make a difference to you when you suffer? If you're not sure about that, keep reading. I hope that as you see how God's knowledge is not only perfect but also personal, it may help you to see things from a new perspective.

When it comes right down to it, what most of us really want to understand about God's omniscience is how it impacts us. We want to know that he knows us—flaws and all. In fact, we want to believe that he knows us intimately—not just the basic facts about us, but the nuances that make us each unique. We want to know that he *does* "know the trouble we've seen."

When I was studying Spanish in high school, I learned two Spanish verbs for *know*—*conocer* and *saber*. *Conocer* is used in reference to people, places, and things; *saber* is used in reference to information. For example, I know (*conocer*) my family, but I know (*saber*) the words to a song. *Conocer* is more relational and intimate than *saber*. God embodies both kinds of knowing. He doesn't just know you like an American citizen knows the president; he knows *you*—intimately. You are significant to God. God's knowledge is perfect, but it helps me to know that his knowledge is also personal. He not only knows when you are singing the blues; he knows why you're singing the blues. He knows what makes you feel like "nobody knows," and he knows how you react when you feel that way. The comforting truth about God's omniscience is that he doesn't just know about you; he knows you.

God Knows You

I wish I hadn't turned on the TV that summer morning. I awoke a little later than usual and knew Phil was already up and the kids were still asleep. So I grabbed the remote and tuned in to *Good*

Morning America. I was just in time to hear an interview with actress Angelina Jolie, who was introduced as one of the most beautiful women in the world. She was starring in a movie in which she played a spy. The interviewer said, "She does her own stunts; she's an amazing mother; she's athletic; she's smart; she's articulate; and she's got a great figure." *Whew!* That's a lot for a girl to wake up to.

I clicked off the TV and heroically performed the only stunt I was capable of—rolling out of bed. When I padded into the kitchen sporting a bed head and faded pj's, Phil greeted me with a cup of coffee. "Thanks, honey," I said. Then I asked, "Did you see that piece on *Good Morning America* about Angelina?" He told me he had. "I bet you like her more than me," I said.

He chuckled as I recounted how pretty she is, what a great figure she has, how smart she is, what a great mom she is, how athletic she is—and on and on I went. I felt insignificant compared to the hot humanitarian I had to digest before breakfast.

Have you ever felt like that? Sure, your trigger may have been different. It may have been an insult from a loved one, a loss of a job you thought you were good at, or a divorce that triggered feelings of insignificance. Many things in life that are far more serious than my moment with Angelina make our hearts lament, "Nobody knows the trouble I've seen," and then wonder, "God, do *you* know?"

Many of us have felt waves of insecurity and insignificance wash over us. But here is the reason I share that glowing testimony about my episode of early morning insecurity: God not only knows everything in a *saber*, informational kind of way; he knows what pushes your buttons and embarrasses you. He knows what hurts you. He knows how you feel and what you think. He knows you have a tendency to compare yourself to supermodels and A-list actresses first thing in the morning and then think really shallow thoughts about what a loser you are. Uh, excuse me, maybe that is just me! Anyway, you get the point. God knows you in a *conocer* kind of way. He doesn't just know about you; he knows *you*. The fact that God is omniscient can have a direct and positive impact on how you perceive yourself, your situations, and your sorrow. His omniscience is perfect, and it is deeply personal.

Think about it. God, by his perfect nature, is the most significant being, and he knows us. He chooses to be completely aware of us—even the small stuff of us! Because he knows you so personally, you can perceive yourself correctly, like he does—wonderfully made and dearly loved. Because he knows your situation so perfectly, you can trust him to work in you in accordance with his good pleasure and will. Because he knows your sorrows personally, you can be assured he will draw near to the brokenhearted and, as the psalmist states, keep each of your tears in his bottle (Psalm 56:8 NLT).

God is aware of everything—and he is especially aware of you.

I love this image from David's psalm: "How precious to me are your thoughts, God! How vast is the sum of them! Were I to count them, they would outnumber the grains of sand" (Psalm 139:17–18). Just how vast is that sum? Well, imagine scooping up a handful of sand and pouring it into a fancy machine that could count every tiny grain. The magical machine tells you your hand can hold 6,000 grains of sand (give or take a few hundred). Now try to imagine how many handfuls of sand might be on one single beach. Then consider how many beaches there are on earth. Before your brain overheats, let me put it like this: God's thoughts toward and about you are astronomically beyond your imagination.

Evidently, they were also beyond David's imagination. "Such knowledge is too wonderful for me," he wrote, "too lofty for me to attain" (Psalm 139:6). And that's my response to God's personal and perfect knowledge as well. It is beautifully and extravagantly beyond my comprehension. What about you?

My friend, you are personally known by God. The God of perfect knowledge is attuned to you and to your every thought and movement. He has searched you, and he knows you. God knows when you sit and when you rise. He perceives your thoughts from afar. He discerns your going out and your lying down. God is familiar with all your ways. Before a word is on your tongue, he knows it completely.

Do you believe what you just read? The words are paraphrased from King David as he recorded them in Psalm 139. God breathed the truth about your significance through David's pen so you could know that you are known and loved by your heavenly Father.

God is fully aware of you. The unfathomable depths and riches of God's knowledge are focused on you because you are known by God. You are significant. In fact, you actually *dwell* in the significance of God. So the next time you think, "Nobody knows the trouble I've seen—and that includes God," the next time you feel God just isn't aware of you or that you are insignificant, tell yourself, "Yes, I am 'in-significant.' I dwell *in* the *significance* of God."

CHAPTER 20

He Knows Your Name

"Before I was born, the LORD called me; from my birth he has made mention of my name."

The prophet Isaiah in Isaiah 49:1 (NIV, 1984 ed.)

Not long ago, I received this e-mail from a woman who subscribes to my monthly e-mail newsletter:

Hi, Jennifer.

I am not sure you will receive this message. You addressing each message with my name makes me feel so warm, and I truly feel you indeed know me. I love reading your messages and visiting your website. Indeed, very encouraging.

Betsy

Betsy's words struck me. Such a small gesture as using her name made such a big impact. The fact that I addressed the newsletter using her name made her feel known. I get that. When someone uses my name, I notice because I feel acknowledged. A name matters.

The nineteenth-century poet and philosopher Henry David Thoreau wrote, "A name pronounced is the recognition of the individual to whom it belongs. He who can pronounce my name aright, he can call me, and is entitled to my love and service." Thoreau penned a truth our hearts intuitively know—if you really know me, you know my name.

If we accept that God is omniscient, we may think his knowledge is so broad that he has the human roll call memorized. Sure, he knows your name, just like he knows fifteen billion other names. But in the way Thoreau phrased it, do you believe he can "pronounce" your name? Is his personal knowledge of you and me what he focuses on? Are you and I really on his mind?

Even King David wondered about this. He wrote, "When I look at the night sky and see the work of your fingers—the moon and the stars you set in place—what are mere mortals that you should think about them, human beings that you should care for them?" (Psalm 8:3–4 NLT). Who are we that God would pay attention and be aware of us individually? Who are we that God should know our names?

The best way I know to think about that question is to use an *anthropomorphism*. Have you ever heard that impressive word? OK, here's what it means so you can casually mention it at dinner and impress your people. To use an anthropomorphism is to give human characteristics to something that is not human. For example, we might say the trees are clapping their hands when the wind blows through their branches, that the family dog is smiling when she wags her tail, or that a house looks sad when it is run-down.

The writer of Proverbs uses an anthropomorphism in describing God: "The eyes of the LORD are everywhere, keeping watch on the wicked and the good" (Proverbs 15:3). The writer uses the metaphor of God's eyes to convey the truth that God knows and is aware of everything and everyone. This doesn't mean that God literally has eyes like we have eyes with corneas and retinas—God is spirit. But as a literary device, assigning human features to God is a way of helping us comprehend God.* The point of saying God's eye is on you is to convey the truth that he knows you.

But then you might wonder, "Is his eye on me in a general, sweeping gaze kind of way, or is it more like a laser? Does he know

---

* Jesus described God as Spirit when he answered a Samaritan woman's question about where to worship God. Jesus said, "God is spirit, and his worshipers must worship in the Spirit and in truth" (John 4:24). He does not have a body as we understand bodies of flesh and blood. We just use human features—like eyes, hands, and hearts—to have a way of relating to him.

my name?" Let's get the prophet Isaiah's take on this, since he beautifully conveys the voice of God. In Scripture, when God uses human characteristics to describe himself, he engages in what scholars call *condescensio*—a Latin word from which we get our English word *condescension*. It describes how assigning human characteristics to God brings God down to our level.

Condescensio is beautifully illustrated when God says through Isaiah, "See, I have engraved you on the palms of my hands; your walls are ever before me" (Isaiah 49:16). So what exactly does this mean? In the culture of Isaiah's day, people sometimes demonstrated their intimate and great love for others by engraving their names on their skin. The Hebrew word we translate "engrave" is *chāqaq* (khaw-kak). It means "to write, or to print." To us, the image of engraving may suggest cutting, but in this verse its meaning is more like writing, marking, or even tattooing. Isaiah uses the picture of God marking us on his palms to help us understand how intimately aware of us God is.

No matter what your stance on tattoos is, think about what Isaiah's image of God represents. You have to be really important to someone if they're willing to go through the pain of being pricked with a tiny needle so they can have a permanent imprint of you on their skin. And that's what God is saying—you are so important to him it's as if he tattooed your name on his hands.

What else does this image convey to you? Can you think of another story in the Bible that describes permanent markings on the palms—the ultimate condescension? Jesus received the marks of crucifixion nails on his palms because he loved you. They left scars that permanently inscribed your name and mine on his hands. Think about it. Tattoos are punctured: "He was pierced for our transgressions" (Isaiah 53:5). And tattoos are permanent: "No one can snatch them out of my Father's hand" (John 10:29).

Knowing Jesus' hands bore the scars of nail punctures, what must the answer be to David's question—"What are mere mortals that [God] should think about them ...?"? I believe the answer is that we must be incredibly valued. It blows my mind! I don't know why

God chooses to be aware of us, much less to know our names, but the glorious truth is, he does.

The sadness you struggle with, the disappointment you carry, your hard past and the trials you endure—he knows. Your best memories, talents, and secret dreams—he knows. Your relationship or the lack of one, your body size and shape—he knows.

My friend, he knows your name. It is ever before him. He can pronounce it perfectly. He truly knows you. Before you were born, he knew your name—it is inscribed on his palms.

You aren't just another set of randomly assembled chromosomes roaming the planet. You are a child of God with a special story and a special calling and a special name. God knows who you are, where you've been, and where you're going. Rest in his intimate knowledge of you.

CHAPTER 21

His Eye Is on You

As for me, I am poor and needy, but the Lord takes thought for me.

The passengers on the bus watched as Susan made her way down the aisle. They saw her place her purse on her lap and collapse her white cane. Some of the regular passengers were familiar with Susan because they had ridden that route for a while and had seen this young woman riding on that bus for about a month. She was thirty-four years old. She had only been blind for a year.

When Susan first lost her sight, she was plunged into a pit of despair. She was filled with fear, terrified about her future. She lost the life she once knew and now had to navigate her new life in darkness. Her husband, Mark, was a good man. He helped her every day, and they worked through the depression, struggles, and fears. It was tough, but she didn't give up. She went through rehabilitative training where she learned to cook, organize her home, navigate her city, and even relearn computer skills—all without sight. And so, after many months, Susan was finally able to return to work.

Mark drove her to the office every morning. He'd park the car, walk her to the door, and kiss her good-bye. They both eased into this routine, and Susan was growing in confidence. However, after several weeks, they both began to sense their routine would have to change. Mark was an officer in the Air Force, and his base was on the opposite side of town. After dropping Susan off, he was having trouble getting there on time. So he finally had to say to her, "Susan, I can't drive you to work anymore. You're going to have to take the bus."

All her fears resurfaced. "I can't take the bus alone! How am I going to learn the routes? How am I going to be safe? How am I going to get from the bus to the office door? You can't leave me!"

"I'm going to ride the bus with you for as long as it takes," Mark promised. "We're going to figure out the route. I'm going to introduce you to the drivers to make sure they take care of you. It's going to be OK. I promise." Reluctantly, Susan conceded, and she and Mark began to ride the bus together. Every day, her confidence grew. And finally, after a month, she threw her arms around Mark, feeling renewed assurance. She was ready to try it on her own.

Monday morning arrived. Mark walked her to the bus stop where she got on the bus and greeted the bus driver she was used to greeting when she and Mark rode. The driver told her where the empty seat was, and she made her way down. On Tuesday morning the same thing occurred. On Wednesday morning a new bus driver was on board, but that was OK because she was pretty confident in what she was doing. She introduced herself. He told her where to sit. Things went great. On Thursday morning the same thing occurred. On Friday morning, as she was getting off the bus, that new bus driver said, "Ma'am, I just have to let you know, it must really feel good to be you."

She was confused. *How in the world could he be talking to me? I'm blind. How could it feel good to be me?* And so she questioned him. "Sir, are you talking to me?" And he said, "Yeah, you just must feel really good to be so well cared for." She was confused. "I don't know what you mean," she said.

"Each day this week that I've seen you," he said, "you get off this bus, and from the time your foot hits the sidewalk, that man over there on the corner in the military uniform watches you, and he never takes his eyes off you. And the whole time you walk, his eyes are on you, and the moment your hand touches the doorknob to go inside your office, he salutes you and walks away."

Her eyes welled up with tears as she thanked the driver. Can you imagine how she felt? She thought she was alone, but she wasn't. She thought no one noticed her, but someone did. Susan never knew her husband's eyes were on her. You and I don't always recognize that God's eyes are on us either.

Have you felt like Susan—alone and unseen? I know I have. Of course, I have literally felt that way. I know what it feels like to be terrified to cross a street alone. I know what it feels like to use every functioning brain cell just to remember where I am walking and to remain oriented. But on a deeper level, I know what it's like to feel despair and fear. And you do too. We all do. And that is when we can feel a deep loneliness.

You may not always be aware that God's eyes are on you. However, even when you don't see him, he sees you. He not only sees you, my friend; he knows you.

Seen by God

A woman who lived thousands of years ago understood what it meant to be seen by God. She was an unnoticed Egyptian slave girl named Hagar. She belonged to Abram's wife, Sarai. Sarai wanted a child and had been promised a child by God, but she hadn't been able to conceive. So since she was about two thousand years away from the nearest fertility clinic, she took matters into her own hands—or, shall I say, she sent Hagar into her husband's tent. And the Bible says, "He slept with Hagar, and she conceived" (Genesis 16:4). What followed was nothing but trouble.

When Hagar became pregnant with Abram's first son, she began to treat Sarai with contempt. Sarai returned the favor—but on steroids! She treated her servant so badly that Hagar finally ran away. When she stopped running, she found herself near a spring of water in the desert. Can you imagine how despondent she must have felt? Alone. Abused. Pregnant. Unseen.

Hagar's anguish was interrupted by a voice she heard coming from near the spring. "Hagar, slave of Sarai, where have you come from, and where are you going?" (Genesis 16:8). It was the voice of the "angel of the LORD," which many Bible scholars consider to be the preincarnate Christ. In other words, God himself appeared to Hagar and called her by name. He saw her, and he knew her.

Not only did God see her; he "heard [her] cry of distress" (Genesis 16:11 NLT). Can you hear his voice calling your name? "Where are you right now? Why are you running? Where is your hope?" Do you realize God sees you and knows what's happening to you? He hears your cry of distress. He is aware of where you are and what you've suffered.

"You are the God who sees me," Hagar said (Genesis 16:13). The Bible uses several Hebrew names for God, and the one Hagar uses here is *El Roi*, which means "the God who sees me."

For God, to see is to know, and to know is to love. And he sees you.

Can You See Him?

You may be dealing with some hard things right now, or perhaps you are carrying the sorrow of someone you love. You may feel unseen by God because all you can see is your sorrow. Sometimes we are so focused on the difficulties surrounding us that we can't see anything else. Sorrow and questions can create an inward focus, a spiritual myopia, that keeps us from seeing anything else. We can become so aware of our own needs and troubles that we inadvertently become unaware of God's presence and attentiveness.

I want to encourage you to become even more aware of how deeply and continuously God sees and knows you. He is *El Roi*. He doesn't have limits to his understanding. He doesn't grow weary of paying attention to you. "Do you not know? Have you not heard? The LORD is the everlasting God, the Creator of the ends of the earth. He will not grow tired or weary, and his understanding no one can fathom" (Isaiah 40:28).

My friend, I know you can grow weary in this life. Sorrows can weigh you down, stress you out, and do you in. But God will never,

never grow weary. He doesn't get heavy eyelids from boredom or fatigue as he watches you. He doesn't blink and miss seeing a tear fall from your eye. When you by faith acknowledge and trust that God knows and sees you, you will feel his strength and experience his comfort. That knowledge can protect you from isolation and despair.

Relying on the truth that God knows can give you confidence to keep trying and trusting. Just like Mark's eyes were on Susan, just like God's eyes were on Hagar, God's eyes are on you. He sees you and knows you and loves you, even when you can't feel it. Perhaps the best question to ask is not, "God, are you aware?" but rather, "God, am *I* aware?"

Are you aware, my friend? I want to be. I need to be reminded that God is fully aware of me. And so do you. So join me in practicing the truth King David gave his son, Solomon: "Acknowledge the God of your father … for the LORD searches every heart and understands every desire and every thought" (1 Chronicles 28:9).

Acknowledge him. How? When you rise, when you sip coffee, acknowledge that he sees you. When you hear the birds sing, when you wipe away a tear, acknowledge that his eyes are on you. When you peel an orange, when you sit by a babbling creek, acknowledge that he sees you in each and every moment. Acknowledge that he knows you and refuses to shift his gaze away from you. When you and I acknowledge God—when we acknowledge who he is and that his eye is on us—we will find such comfort in the truth that he really does understand our desires and know our thoughts. And the God of perfect knowledge has perfect love for you, my friend. His eye has always been, and will always be, on you.

CHAPTER 22

Tell God What He Already Knows

> Be sure that the ins and outs of your individuality are no mystery to him; and one day they will no longer be a mystery to you.
>
> C. S. Lewis, *The Problem of Pain*

During the season I was in the thick of depression, I spiraled into a place of deep doubt. I doubted God's existence and the deity of Christ. I questioned the Bible and all the truths I once held dear. But even in my doubts, I wrestled with God, often using my journal to pray out my confusion:

> God, I do not understand you. I don't want to question your existence, so why am I? If you weren't real, I wouldn't be here. I get nervous when I think of the Bible being flawless too. It was written and compiled by flawed human beings—I don't want to doubt whether or not it is perfect. I really don't. I don't want to dishonor you, even though I am so uncertain about all the beliefs I have taken for granted for years.
>
> I do believe. I think I do. Help my unbelief.
>
> It is becoming so clear to me that what this painful journey is really about is my spiritual blindness, not my physical blindness.

When I reread my journal now, I think I was far more alarmed about my doubts than God was. I wanted to avoid the pain of my confusion and feelings of loss, but God mercifully allowed me to feel them. God already knew I was struggling, and he was aware of every nuance of my heart and mind. I believed him enough to tell him of my doubts, even though I wasn't sure he was real. I was so confused, but I had just enough hope and volition to hang on to what I couldn't understand. After several terrifying months, God's grace gently guided me back to the truth that he did not call himself "I Feel" or "I Think," but "I Am."

We all have times of spiritual questions, confusion, or doubt. Sometimes we think it's shameful to doubt, or perhaps it's an indictment on our faith if we ask questions. But God knows what is in our hearts. He is fully aware when we are struggling. We sometimes try to hide our questions from others, and even ourselves, because our questions and doubts make us feel insecure or ashamed. But far worse is when we try to hide them from God.

There is no reason to hide our questions from God because "the Lord does not look at the things people look at. People look at the outward appearance, but the Lord looks at the heart" (1 Samuel 16:7). God sees right through your fears, insecurity, questions, and doubts and perceives your heart. He knows what you are feeling and thinking. And he is not alarmed, offended, or shocked by your doubts and questions. In fact, he has had some experience in that area! He has dealt with people who have a lot of doubt and a little faith. So just be honest. That's what Thomas did.

Honest Thomas

When the disciples were gathered together, consoling one another after Jesus' death, the resurrected Christ appeared to them (John 20:19–20). Although the door was locked, Jesus was suddenly among them. All the disciples were astonished, but one was missing. He has come to be known as "doubting Thomas." But I sometimes wonder if that is what God called him. Could we perhaps call him "honest Thomas" instead?

On Friday, Thomas saw Jesus die. On Saturday, he must have battled sorrow, anger, and confusion all day long. On Sunday,

Thomas surely caught wind that Jesus' tomb was found empty. On Sunday evening, he didn't join his friends for their meal—but the risen Christ did. When the other disciples told Thomas that Jesus had been with them, that he truly was risen, Thomas basically stated, "I have to see it to believe it."

Have you lived through a time of trial or a season of life when you felt like Thomas?

Friday: Thomas's hopes were crucified on the cross. Do you know how he felt? You lose something precious to you—a dream, a relationship, your health, your sense of purpose or security. Your hopes are shattered, and life suddenly isn't what you expected.

Saturday: Thomas is stunned, shocked, and grief stricken—Jesus had died. It wasn't supposed to turn out this way. Perhaps you know how he felt because you find yourself in the aftershock of disappointment or tragedy. You are stuck in a hard place and overwhelmed by sadness and confusion. What you hoped for didn't happen, or what you prayed would not happen did. You aren't sure what to do, but you know for certain that your life will never be the same.

Sunday: Thomas hears from his friends that Jesus is alive. Why can't he feel as certain or happy as everyone else? What is wrong with him? And maybe you understand this part of Thomas's story as well. All your friends have a happiness you don't. You envy their hopes and the way their lives look so peaceful compared to yours. It seems so easy for some people to trust God, but for you, it's just not that easy. You want the security and hope they have, yet you can't shake your doubts or settle the grinding confusion in your heart. You want to believe, but you just can't.

It's OK if you have felt like Thomas, or if you do right now. All of us experience the "I have to see it to believe it" state of mind at some point.

In his despair and disillusionment, Thomas could have turned his back on everything. But he stays connected with his friends and shows up for supper with the disciples a week later. Jesus again appears among his followers. Once more, he enters through a locked door and greets them with the words, "Peace be with you!" (John 20:26). Jesus holds out his scarred hands for Thomas to examine. He opens his outer garment and says to Thomas, "Reach out your hand and put it into my side." In awe, Thomas drops to his knees and exclaims, "My Lord and my God!" (John 20:27–28).

Jesus knew Thomas had questions and doubts. Jesus didn't scold Thomas or shame him for not being as trusting as his friends were. He simply offered Thomas a chance to experience him as the risen Christ in a very personal way—he let Thomas feel his scars. Jesus was willing to reveal himself to Thomas, even though Thomas was doubtful. And that's what Jesus does for all of us; he gives us himself.

God Reveals Himself to Us in Our Questions

Questions don't always reveal answers, but your questions will reveal Christ.

Because God is fully aware of you, because he knows you completely, he knows where you struggle. He knows the hidden doubts you may harbor about him. And he wants you to know he knows. Perhaps, like he did for Thomas, he is extending his arms to you right now through the pages of this book. Perhaps the quiet nudge you feel in your spirit as you consider his truths is his way of inviting you to reach out and touch him.

Thomas's questions and doubts could have led him away from the Christ he loved and away from his friends who followed the Christ. But what a loss that would have been. Your questions and doubt can take you many places if you let them. They can take you down a road of cynicism, despair, or loneliness. But, my friend, what a waste of your doubts and questions! When you are full of questions and doubt, might you respond like Thomas? Might you stay connected with your friends who follow Christ? Will you take whatever faith or curiosity you have and channel it toward Christ himself? He welcomes questions, and he welcomes the questioner. He already knows your questions, but ask him anyway. Jesus won't just give you the lesser gift of an answer; Jesus will give you himself because he is the answer.

Thomas's pain, confusion, and doubt didn't keep him from experiencing Jesus in a deeper, more personal way. In fact, it was his doubt and pain that drew him to get as close as possible to Jesus. It was in the midst of Thomas's honest struggles that Jesus revealed himself to Thomas. He will do that for you too.

Don't hide your questions from God; he knows they are in your heart anyway. He is not thrown off by your doubts; he knows what you struggle to understand. He is not ready to pounce as soon as you tell him what he already knows. He knows, and he loves. We should ask God questions. When we do, he opens his hands to us and allows us to experience the reality of his presence. My friend, what you most long for is not proof of Jesus' reality, but rather, the reality of Jesus' presence.

If you're struggling with questions or uncomfortable feelings about faith and God, tell him. He already knows. When you are willing to reveal yourself completely to God, he reveals himself to you.

CHAPTER 23

Forgetful Omniscience

What is forgiven is usually well remembered.

Louis Dudek

My hand was on the door handle, ready to open the stall and leave the bathroom. But then I heard familiar voices and stood perfectly still. The Sunday worship service was about to begin, and two women from the church were standing at the sink talking about our pastor while washing their hands. They thought they were alone. Their comments about him were small and mean. They took turns criticizing the pastor's sermon, his tie, and even his hair. I was so angry I could barely breathe. It's one thing to overhear cutting remarks about someone you respect, and it's another thing entirely when that person is also your dad.

I hid inside the stall until I heard them leave. I felt so hurt and betrayed. I wished I could forget what I had just heard about my dad, but I could not. I joined the two sister saints in the sanctuary for worship and listened to them sing with the choir about Jesus, including words about "his grace" and "his forgiveness."

To this day, I wish I'd had the nerve to swing that door wide open and give a big cheery "Hello!" to the dastardly duo. Then they would have felt as miserable as I was feeling, though for altogether different reasons. Trust me, their hands were not what needed to be washed. If my no-nonsense grandmother had been there, two somebodies would have had their mouths washed out with soap!

I prayed a lot for my dad during that time because the bathroom conversation was just a symptom of a larger problem growing in our congregation. A group of disagreeables were saying awful things about my dad and treating him badly. *God, are you aware? Have you forgotten about my dad? Have you not noticed his integrity and faithfulness? Can you not see how nasty these people are being? Are you going to let them get away with saying such awful things?*

Unfortunately, it was not the kind of situation that quickly resolved itself. In fact, it lasted a whole year—a really long year. It lasted so long that it felt like God really had forgotten about it—and us too. Sure, I knew God was all-knowing. But that character quality of God didn't seem to be helping us. I think when we feel alone like that, we can wonder if God just gets distracted. Maybe he is aware but preoccupied? Or maybe he just forgets?

Can God Forget?

Does an omniscient God even have the ability to forget? You may think so, if you've read some of the prayers people prayed in the Bible. For example, Hannah, David, and Asaph all begged God not to forget.

- Hannah: "LORD Almighty, if you will only look on your servant's misery and remember me, and not forget your servant but give her a son, then I will give him to the LORD for all the days of his life." (1 Samuel 1:11)
- David: "Arise, LORD! Lift up your hand, O God. Do not forget the helpless." (Psalm 10:12)
- Asaph: "Remember how the enemy has mocked you, LORD, how foolish people have reviled your name. Do not hand over the life of your dove to wild beasts; do not forget the lives of your afflicted people forever ... Do not ignore the clamor of your adversaries, the uproar of your enemies, which rises continually." (Psalm 74:18–19, 23)

These three people of faith asked God to remember, to not forget. Why would they pray about such a thing unless it was possible that God might forget them? How does God explain this? Well, we will hear his explanation in a bit, but first let's hear what he has to say about this whole matter of being forgetful.

According to Scripture, God says he does not forget because he is merciful and keeps his oaths (Deuteronomy 4:31). And the author of Hebrews affirms, "God is not unjust; he will not forget your work and the love you have shown him as you have helped his people and continue to help them" (Hebrews 6:10). In the Bible, God clearly reveals himself as one who notices everything and forgets nothing. He didn't forget Hannah, David, Asaph, or my dad—and he will never forget you.

There is nothing God can't do, for he is limitless in power. He chooses to remember; he chooses not to forget. He regards you, and he knows your situation. Your adversity does not escape his notice. My friend, God hasn't forgotten you. He hasn't forgotten your pain, frustration, or any detail of your life. However, there is one thing he *has* chosen to forget. God declared, "I, even I, am he who blots out your transgressions, for my own sake, and remembers your sins no more" (Isaiah 43:25). Did you catch that? The God who knows everything and forgets nothing chooses *not* to remember our sins. I love that! In fact, the psalmist writes, "As far as the east is from the west, so far has he removed our transgressions from us" (Psalm 103:12).

I believe God inspired David to use the image of east and west when he wrote that psalm because north and south are a finite distance apart, whereas east and west are an infinite distance apart. If you're traveling north, you will eventually cross the North Pole and begin traveling south again. This doesn't happen when you're traveling east or west, and thus the distance between us and our sins is infinite. It's an especially powerful metaphor when you consider David wrote this psalm at a time when people thought the world was flat with four corners. David wouldn't have known that the distance between east and west was infinite; he just thought it was far.

In the original context, the literary use of east and west functions as a merism. OK, so when I looked it up and learned about it, I had to tell you about it, since if you're like me, you may not know what it means. A merism is a figure of speech that combines a pair of contrasting words to describe the whole of something. For example, high and low, young and old, near and far. Get it? So east and west are opposites, yet in their contrast we see a complete picture of what God is saying. Our sins are so far removed from us that they vanish.

We can't grasp an infinite distance, but God can. So if this is God we're talking about—a God who has infinite and perfect knowledge—how can our sin be lost to him? Here's the best way I know to think about this. Imagine God has a computerlike mind and his "memory" is complete—no data needs to be added, and none can be deleted. So how could God possibly forget our sin? Isn't everything about us stored in his memory? Does he somehow press a divine delete key? I am no Bill Gates, but my understanding is that nothing is ever truly deleted from a computer hard drive. A skilled and motivated computer geek can always retrieve deleted information. So when I think about how God forgets our sins, I don't think it's accurate to say our sin is "deleted." I think it's more accurate to say that God chooses not to retrieve our sins. God doesn't keep our sin in a readily accessible file on his desktop; instead he archives it in infinity, never to be retrieved again. He removes our sin as far as the east is from the west.

Forgetting and Remembering

But the question remains: If God doesn't forget, why did people throughout the Bible ask God *not* to forget, or specifically request that he *remember*? Ready for the explanation? OK, OK. Here we go ...

When Scripture uses the word *remember* in connection with God, it isn't an, "Oh yeah, I forgot!" kind of remembering. It conveys attentiveness or kind regard. For example, when the text states

"God remembered Rachel" (Genesis 30:22), it doesn't mean that, after briefly forgetting her, God suddenly remembers her. It means he showed her kind regard. When we read that God "remembered his covenant with Abraham, with Isaac and with Jacob" (Exodus 2:24), it doesn't mean he said something like, "Oh yeah, how could I have forgotten?" It means he acknowledged and affirmed his covenant.

It is this sense of the word *remember* as attentiveness and kind regard that is the key to answering the question we asked earlier: "Why did people like Hannah, David, and Asaph ask God not to forget them?" The answer: They are simply praying, "Regard me, Lord. Take heed of my plight."

God does not forget you; he regards you. Yet he does forget your sin. So what is it you've done or thought that you wish God wasn't aware of? What mistakes have you made or bad choices are in your past that you wish God just wasn't able to know about? We all have stuff, but if you have asked God for forgiveness, then he can't remember your stuff. None of us have a flawless past, but the good news is that an all-knowing God chooses to "forget" our forgiven sins, bad choices, and rebellions. He does not call them to mind.

God is aware of you; he knows you and regards you as worthy of his attention. Although God knows you and everything about you, he chooses not to remember your sin. And that's not a contradiction—it's just flat-out amazing!

God can disregard our sin because Jesus already dealt with it for us. God regarded it on Calvary once and for all. The reason your sin is never retrieved from God's memory is because God's "screensaver" is a picture of his Son on your cross.

O God, thank you for your forgetful omniscience.

CHAPTER 24

God, Am I Aware?

Silence sits immense upon my soul. Then comes hope with a smile and whispers, "There is joy in self-forgetfulness." So I try to make the light in others' eyes my sun, the music in others' ears my symphony, the smile on others' lips my happiness.

Helen Keller, *The Story of My Life*

The summer during my depression, Phil tried to cheer me up by throwing a surprise half-birthday party. Actually, it was a half-birthday party minus one month. You see, my real birthday, the one God gave me, is December 19. But several years ago, I decided I was no longer celebrating on that day because it was too stressful. You know, Christmas shopping, parties, baking, traveling—no time to celebrate my birthday that close to Jesus' big day. So I decided to celebrate my half birthday six months earlier. But the problem was, I miscalculated. Instead of choosing June 19, I chose July 19. Oh well!

So on that July 19, Phil invited some of our closest friends for dinner and asked each to bring a musical birthday card. Great idea, huh? Well, in theory it was, but when you are depressed, a party is a bad, bad, bad idea. But at that point, I'd honed my ability to fake it into an art form, so I used all my energy to smile and be gracious. As we sat in a circle while I opened cards, everything felt sluggish and thick. The envelope seals took a week to open. I could only move in slow motion. Truly, my brain was so foggy and my feelings so fuzzy that I was just a mess inside. But two things stand out in my memories of that night. One, I felt fat. But that is not the point. I just thought I would share. I really didn't want to sit there and eat cake when I already felt like a Goodyear blimp. But the other thing that stands out is the light and happy sound of the voices around the circle as they laughed and chatted and wished me happy birthday. I remember thinking, *You don't even know me. If you really knew me, you wouldn't be here. You would know I am in a pit and barely capable of even sitting here without crying. Phil doesn't really know me. None of you do.* I felt so misunderstood—like even the people closest to me had no idea who I really was.

Now, before you think I was totally self-absorbed, let me tell you that my reaction was definitely the irrational vocabulary of depression. I could have been honest with my friends and invited them into my darkness. But I wasn't honest, and I didn't invite them in. However, even if my perspective was irrational, it was real. I truly felt like no one was really aware of me—the real me.

In the midst of depression, my world got smaller, and consequently my problems seemed bigger. And that's often what happens when I struggle. I can unintentionally become more self-focused, even though I know intellectually that I am the happiest when I am the most self-forgetful. It's hard to not focus on myself when I'm suffering. It seems to take all my energy just to keep myself from losing hope. And perhaps you're nodding your head right now because you know what I'm talking about—you've been there too. So, how do we deal with this uncomfortable reality? Can we grow in our awareness of God and consequently become less self-focused when we struggle?

Shifting Focus

Before Jesus began his public ministry, there was a well-known preacher whom many people came to hear. He was what we might call a man's man—tough, rugged, no-nonsense. However, personally, I can't imagine a woman who would want to hang out with him because he was known for eating nasty things like locusts and wild honey. And he had a very bad fashion sense, always wearing some tuniclike thing made from camel's hair and accented with a leather belt. He probably didn't smell very good, and I can imagine his hair looked a bit unruly. But this man was considered one of the greatest men ever born. Scripture prophesied that he would have a unique role in preparing the way for Messiah. His name was John the Baptist.

John the Baptist took center stage in his day—he was well-known, was the topic of many conversations, and had devoted disciples. But then came one who was greater than him—one of whom John said, "I'm not worthy even to be his slave and carry his sandals" (Matthew 3:11 NLT). When Jesus approached the Jordan River and asked John to baptize him, the focus of attention shifted. John said, "He must increase, but I must decrease" (John 3:30 NASB). In other words, John the Baptist was eager and willing to have the focus on Jesus rather than on himself.

Now, I don't mention John because he was in the middle of a trial or rough time at this point in his life—he wasn't. But his example is relevant to us when we are in a trial or tough time. Here's why. He didn't say, "He must increase, but I must disappear." He didn't say, "He must increase, but I must become completely irrelevant." Note the precision of the statement: "He must increase, but I must decrease." It's a shift of focus. We do not ignore our pain or dismiss our sorrow. We do not neglect or debase ourselves. We just shift our focus. Instead of focusing on me and me alone, I glance at me and gaze at Jesus. We could apply John's words to our own lives by seeking to become less focused on ourselves and our circumstances and more focused on God.

Becoming more aware of God helps us recognize how very aware of our situations he truly is. It begins to free us from the chains of sorrow and bitterness. But how do we do that in real life? In an everyday, practical way, how can we reduce our self-focus and grow in our God-focus? Well, maybe applying these three R's will help—recognize, replace, and regard.

1. Recognize "I"

Pay attention to how often you think or say "I."

Self-focus is a habit. We develop it quite naturally, and it is a supernatural feat to recognize it and break the habit. Now, do not misunderstand. You absolutely should think "I" thoughts — that is healthy and expected. But having an overabundance of "I" thoughts, and having them in exclusion of any "God" or "others" thoughts, isn't healthy. Ask God to awaken you to how often you think and say "I."

"I like," "I want," "I think," "I wish," and "I feel" are words we use to begin a statement. Anything that has to do with our needs, desires, and opinions begins with the letter *I*. So how do we pay attention to and recognize how often we say and think "I"? One way is to focus on asking questions rather than making statements. Here are a couple examples of what I mean:

- "Do you like this coffee?" instead of "I don't like this coffee."
- "What would Jesus do if the woman who just insulted me insulted him?" instead of "I am so insulted right now that I am about to throw a pity party where I am the guest of honor and I get to eat all the cake while I cry about how unfair my life is."

OK, those are simplified examples, but you get the idea. Training your brain to not think "I" first will keep you from ending up alone on your own "I-land" of despair. Becoming aware of how self-focused you are is the first step toward becoming more God-focused.

2. Replace "I" with "God"

When you recognize that you are becoming preoccupied with "I" statements or indulging in I-focused thoughts, counter them with "God" statements. When you say "I feel," follow it with "God says." For example, follow a statement like "I feel like no one knows me" with "God says he sees and knows me. He sees when I sit and when I stand, when I lie down and when I rise."

When you can't get beyond "I want" thoughts, follow them with "God gives" statements. When you think "I want relief from this heaviness" or "I want to be healed," follow it with "God gives me a garment of praise I can wear when I am dealing with such heaviness" or "God gives me sufficient grace, whether I am to remain blind or be healed."

I am not saying this is easy—it isn't. But it is possible. "All things are possible with God" (Mark 10:27). With God's help, you can train your heart, mind, and spirit to follow your "I" statements with "God" statements. Eventually, you will develop the habit of thinking "God" before "I"—and that is when you begin to experience true freedom and contentment.

3. Regard Others

Paul gave this instruction to the church in Philippi: "In humility value others above yourselves" (Philippians 2:3). However, what he did not advise them to do is disregard or devalue themselves. He wasn't telling them to ignore their legitimate needs or treat themselves as if they didn't matter. Rather, he was telling them—and us—to make the needs and best interests of others a primary concern. I love how *The Message* clarifies this point in Paul's instruction: "Don't be obsessed with getting your own advantage. Forget yourselves long enough to lend a helping hand" (Philippians 2:4 MSG). When we forget ourselves in this way, we begin to think of others as worthy of our interest and care; we consider them even more important than we are.

I have seen a friend practice this, and oh how it has helped her in her own pain. She was struggling with loneliness and feelings of rejection because her husband of twenty years walked out on her. She began to volunteer at a teen homeless shelter and weekly served meals and helped them with their laundry. Most importantly, she just hung out with them. It helped her shift her gaze from her own problems and gain a broader view; it helped keep her own pain in perspective. This mind-set will help us to more consistently regard others and their needs. It levels the playing field of sorrow and suffering. As we see others' needs as important, ours morph into their proper size.

When we recognize how often we indulge in "I" thoughts, and as we begin to replace "I" thoughts with "God" thoughts, it does result in an eagerness on our part to regard others. And when we are more focused on others and their needs, we become less focused on our own. There really is healing and freedom when the letter "I" shrinks to size. In fact, becoming less self-focused can protect us from becoming more selfish.

Suffering and Selfishness

Here's the hard truth: suffering can bring out our selfishness. If you aren't selfish, then I need you to come to my house and mentor me. Just when I think I am not very selfish, something crops up to show me I am wrong. My friend, here's the dark truth about selfish people: they suffer harder. That is why I bring this up. Being too self-focused makes every sorrow deeper, every problem bigger, and every slight more personal. It harms us and makes us forget God and others.

So let's consider how differently my almost half-birthday party might have been if I had recognized how self-absorbed I was.

When I was focused on thoughts about how my friends didn't really know me, I could have followed those thoughts with a God-centered thought like "God knows me." I could have moved the spotlight off of me and my perception and focused it on others. "They are so kind to be here for me. My friends took time away from their needs and obligations and spent it with me."

I could have regarded them and their needs as more important than mine. "I wonder what is behind their eyes. I wonder if some heartbreak is behind their smiles, and some tears hidden behind their laughter. How can I make them feel special and appreciated?"

Now, I don't know if I could have done those things while I was so low and confused, but if someone had coached me, I might have had a better chance. That's why I share this with you. I don't know how you are feeling or why you are reading this book. I don't know the nature of your struggle or the questions you have. But I do know that God is completely and compassionately aware of you. He wants you to rest in the knowledge of his awareness. Perhaps my almost half-birthday pit—I mean *party*—can help you become more aware of God and others so you can weather your storm with a little more joy.

Making these mental, spiritual, and emotional shifts won't solve the problems we face, but doing so truly will help us to decrease so that God can increase. And when we are more aware of God and others than we are of ourselves, we will experience greater peace and contentment.

Threads of Truth for Your Blanket of Faith

- Nothing in all creation is hidden from God's sight. Everything is uncovered and laid bare before the eyes of him to whom we must we must give account. (Hebrews 4:13)
- Even the darkness will not be dark to you; the night will shine like the day, for darkness is as light to you. (Psalm 139:12)
- "Now we can see that you know all things and that you do not even need to have anyone ask you questions. This makes us believe that you came from God." (John 16:30)
- "I know the plans I have for you ..." (Jeremiah 29:11)
- The LORD will work out his plans for my life—for your faithful love, O LORD, endures forever. Don't abandon me, for you made me. (Psalm 138:8 NLT)
- The LORD will guide you always; he will satisfy your needs in a sun-scorched land and will strengthen your frame. You will be like a well-watered garden, like a spring whose waters never fail. (Isaiah 58:11)

Visit jenniferrothschild.com/threads to download free Scripture cards.

PART 6

God, Are You There?

Everything was perfect for our vacation. The sun was bright and warm; the breeze on the beach was lovely; the rhythm of the ocean's waves crashing onto the shore created a soothing soundtrack I normally love to hear. But instead of being outside, I was holed up in our rented condo, which felt dark and damp, and where the only sounds were the scratchy hum of the refrigerator and the dull whoosh of the air conditioner.

I was surrounded by family, but I felt alone.

That afternoon, I could have gone to the pool with Phil. But I would have just sat alone on a beach chair while he swam, so I decided to stay inside. At least in the condo I could type and talk to my invisible companion—my computer. And thanks to author Jules Verne and my MP3 player, I did have the fine company of Captain Nemo and the boys from the submarine *Nautilus*. What would I do without the friendship of my books?

I was listening to *Twenty Thousand Leagues Under the Sea*, my vacation novel. I had just finished the part of the story where the *Nautilus* is heading toward a great ice barrier. The narrator describes it as a desolate expanse where "everything was frozen, even sound." The image caught me off guard, and I pressed the pause button.

Frozen sound. I know exactly what that's like. I may be surrounded by people on a warm beach, but my insides feel like an empty cavern where the only sound I hear is the frozen echo of "alone," "alone," "alone."

I contemplated that word—*alone*. I realized I didn't so much mind being physically alone, but I hated feeling emotionally and spiritually alone. I got up from the wicker rocking chair and set the MP3 player on the cushion to walk to the kitchen for a glass of peach tea. As I filled my glass, I could hear the seagulls squawking outside. They didn't sound alone. Theirs was not a desolate expanse but a boundless, welcoming sky where they flew in freedom. It was a thought that made me feel even more alone; I had no companions in the vast dark sky I was navigating. The ice cubes clinked in my glass as I walked back to the rocker and picked up my MP3 player.

At twenty thousand leagues below sea level, the ice fields were now so thick and treacherous the *Nautilus* was forced to halt its brave journey. A passenger named Ned was concerned that Captain Nemo might nevertheless try to go farther. "Nobody can clear the Ice Bank," he said to Dr. Aronnax, a scientist and the protagonist in the story. "Your captain's a powerful man, but ... he isn't more powerful than nature. If she draws a boundary line, there you stop, like it or not!"

"Correct," Dr. Aronnax agreed but also admitted, "I still want to know what's behind this Ice Bank! Behold my greatest source of irritation—a wall!" Then Conseil, the doctor's assistant, made a statement that struck a deep chord in me: "All walls should be banned." I hit the pause button again.

I may as well be twenty thousand leagues under the sea—that's pretty much how far away I feel from everyone right now, even God. Blindness is my Ice Bank, my wall, and depression makes it feel even more overwhelming. Everything inside me is screaming, "All walls should be banned! Get me out of here!" Nothing infuriates me more than a wall I can't get around. It just makes me feel so trapped and alone. But I am stuck here in this desolation.

Blindness had never been easy, but that summer it became an oppressive, unyielding barrier. I felt imprisoned, emotionally and spiritually. And I battled the fear that this was not only my present but my future—that I would always be trapped in this horrible confinement. I was numb and exhausted, and I just wanted out.

Blindness is a wall I know I will never get over. The only way out is if God picks me up and carries me.

God, are you there?

CHAPTER 25

AWOL

*Let a man think and care ever so little about God, he does not
therefore exist without God. God is here with him, upholding,
warming, delighting, and teaching him—making life a good
thing to him. God gives him himself, though the man knows
it not.*

George MacDonald, "The Consuming Fire"

Not long ago, Phil and I were sitting in a coffee shop comforting our friend David, who was in shock and utterly heartbroken because his wife had just left him. Fighting back tears, he said, "On top of everything else, I don't feel God's presence. I feel completely alone."

Maybe you understand what David was experiencing. Any time something bad happens, it often leaves us feeling profoundly lonely. You may be married or surrounded by friends, but when the doctor gives you a cancer diagnosis, you are keenly aware that you are alone with the disease. If you suffer from depression or other mental illness, it can feel like there is no one else in the world who understands what you're going through. And anyone who has lost a spouse knows what it's like to be pitched into a canyon of grief that no one experiences as deeply as you do. Suffering, in whatever form it comes, can make us feel so incredibly alone. And it only compounds the hardship when it seems that God, too, is absent— or what I sometimes refer to as A-W-O-L (absent without love).

That feeling of God's absence reminds me a little of what it feels like to be blind. I don't mean blind in a spiritual sense. I mean that blindness is a good metaphor of what it feels like to be alone, even when you're not. I've had times when someone is standing nearby me, but if they're not talking or moving, I have no way to know they're there. And if they're quiet while I'm talking to them, I am never 100 percent sure they haven't walked away while I am midsentence! That can make me feel insecure, alone, or isolated. How strange that I feel those emotions even when someone is right there with me. I feel alone, but my feelings offer no reliable confirmation that I actually am alone. And we can experience something similar with God—feeling distant from him and unaware of his presence, even though he is right there.

I surely don't want to simplify the profound nature of God, nor do I want to minimize the pain you may be in if God feels absent right now. But, my friend, sometimes you, we, have to *trust* God is there, even when we can't *feel* him.

God Is Near

There is a brief Old Testament passage that helps me trust that God is with me, even when it feels like he is absent. Speaking through the prophet Jeremiah, God poses three questions to reveal the truth about who he is and where he is present:

> *"Am I a God who is only close at hand?" says the* Lord.
> *"No, I am far away at the same time.*
> *Can anyone hide from me in a secret place?*
> *Am I not everywhere in all the heavens and earth?"*
> *says the* Lord.
>
> Jeremiah 23:23–24 NLT

God makes it clear he is near to all, able to be everywhere so no one can hide from him—in fact, he fills the very space that surrounds us. He is with you right now. You don't have a small piece of God or receive only an occasional visit from God—you have all of God with you, always. He is 100 percent present, 100 percent of the time, with 100 percent of the people. Whew!

God is everywhere. The theological term for this reality is "omnipresent." *Omni* is from the Latin word *omnis*, meaning "all"; *present* means "at hand" and "in attendance"—the opposite of absent. Yet even a big, smart-sounding word like *omnipresent* doesn't do justice to the huge concept that God is everywhere and with everyone at all times. It is really hard to wrap our finite minds around such a huge concept, isn't it?

God Is Like ...

I don't know about you, but when I'm wrestling with a tough issue, it often helps if I can talk it through with someone. So when I was wrestling to understand the truth that God is always with us, I called my friend Lisa. I asked her to finish this sentence: *God is like* _____.

"God is like air," she said without hesitation.

"Air? Did you just think of that?" I asked, surprised she had such a quick, good, and profound answer.

"Yes!" She laughed. "Air is everywhere in our daily lives. We can't go anywhere that it is not. We all breathe it."

Think about it. Air is what we all need to survive. We have different languages and skin colors, but we have air in common. It is everywhere. It is invisible, and most times, we don't even think about it and our need for it.

Air is perceptible when it rustles the leaves on a tree or comes in gusts or a cyclone. We notice air when it's blustery on a wintery day or weighted with humidity in July. Perhaps it's easy to think about God's omnipresence in the way we think of air because he is as near and essential as air—our native breath. Not surprisingly, God's very name suggests something similar.

Through the prophet Isaiah, God said, "I am the Lord; that is my name! I will not yield my glory to another or my praise to idols" (Isaiah 42:8). Whenever you see the word Lord in small capital letters in your Bible, it refers to this proper name for God rendered in Hebrew with four letters, YHWH (which we pronounce as "Yahweh"). The Greek word for this sacred reference to God is *tetragrammaton*, which simply means "four letters." Appearing over 6,800 times, YHWH is the most common name used for God in Scripture.

Out of deep reverence and respect for God, YHWH was considered unpronounceable, and so it was only written and never spoken. A Greek translation of the Old Testament rendered the *tetragrammaton* using the word *Kyrios*, which means "Lord." Many biblical scholars believe YHWH also conveyed the idea of "breath" or "life." A similar meaning is evidenced in the name God uses for himself when speaking with Moses through the burning bush. God says, "I AM WHO I AM" (Exodus 3:14). The Semitic root of this name, *hawah*, means "to be" or "to become." It represents a present, active God. In ancient Hebrew thought, this sense of God's identity as "I AM" or "to be" may have been fused with "breath" or "life," resulting in a larger meaning similar to Life-Giver or Creator.

Got that?

Here's the significance of all those definitions. The Bible states it plainly: "For the LORD is your life" (Deuteronomy 30:20). In other words, he is not merely a part of your life—he created you; he is the reason you are alive, the source of your very breath. Isn't it amazing to think that God names himself in a way that reminds us we cannot exist without him? I love that!

This same truth is communicated in the New Testament through the apostle Paul. In describing the ever-present God to a group of intellectuals and philosophers gathered in Athens, Paul said of God, "In him we live and move and have our being" (Acts 17:28). The God who breathed life into Adam is the same God who gives us the breath of life. God's breath not only sustains our lives, but our very lives are in his hands. Simply put, without him, we would not exist. YHWH is life. He is I AM. He is as present as the air you breathe. He is as near as the very air that surrounds you—only nearer. He is there, even when you can't feel his presence. He is not "I FEEL," but "I AM." He isn't merely important to your life; he *is* your life.

My friend, God is never AWOL. It is impossible for his presence or love to be absent. Does this truth connect with you? Do you realize he is that present? Take a moment right now and inhale deeply, and as you do, breathe in his name — *Yahweh*. He is as present as the air you just breathed. Now exhale, and as you do, breathe out his name again — *Yahweh*. He is I AM, and because he is, you are never alone. Because he is, you *are*.

CHAPTER 26

Hide-and-Seek

Where can I go from your Spirit? Where can I flee from your presence?... When I awake, I am still with you.

Psalm 139:7, 18

Close your eyes for a moment and imagine you are in a swimming pool. Uh, I guess that won't really work since you need to keep your eyes open to read! (These are the details I forget about you sighted people; you need to keep your eyes open to see!) Anyway, picture this with me. You are paddling in the deep end of a refreshing pool (located in the perfectly manicured backyard of your mansion). Your eyes are tightly shut and you say, "Marco!" You wait to hear another swimmer say ... what? Yep, I heard you— you said, "Polo!" Remember what the point of that game is? The unfortunate player squawking "Marco" is "it." This swimmer has to try to find all the other sneaky swimmers by following their voices when they answer, "Polo!" It's a game that can drive a person crazy because, just when you think you are about to tag someone because you heard them close by and know they are there, you reach out and they're gone! It's a maddening game of hide-and-seek that reminds us how frustrating it is when people hide from us.

Now, that's just a game, but what about when you feel like you are drowning in the deep end of life and you call out for divine help. "God," you pray, and he responds, "Right here." Then you swim toward him only to discover he's not where you thought he was, and it seems like he's actually hiding from you.

The psalmist knew exactly what that felt like. He asked God, "Why, LORD, do you stand far off? Why do you hide yourself in times of trouble?" (Psalm 10:1). The psalmist even accuses God of dozing off: "Awake, Lord! Why do you sleep? Rouse yourself! Do not reject us forever. Why do you hide your face and forget our misery and oppression?" (Psalm 44:23–24).

Though those passages reflect a true heart cry for God to say "Polo" when we say "Marco," a desire for God to be there instead of hide, the psalmists seem to understand that God's presence is not the opposite of his absence. Did you get that? In other words, just because we can't sense his presence, it doesn't mean he is absent. Sometimes it seems God really does "hide" or is intentional about cloaking his presence. How do we account for this?

Smarter minds with seminary degrees boil it down to a few reasons. Some believe God hides because he wants our faith to grow. Others think God hides because he loves us and wants us to seek him. And still others point out that God isn't the one hiding; we just can't sense him because our sin separates us from God. It's this last reason that interests me most. Why? Because even if we understood precisely why God sometimes hides his presence, it wouldn't bring us comfort. In those times, we just have to trust that God is out to do us good, whether or not we can feel it. But when God's absence is a result of our decisions rather than his, we need to consider another perspective. Maybe when God seems absent, it's not because *he's* hiding but because *we* are.

Hiding from God

When I was a girl, we adopted a white toy poodle named Cannoli. I don't know why her former family named her after an Italian pastry; maybe she reminded them of that yummy filling. Cannoli was a puffy, fluffy ball of white fur. She was adorable, but she didn't look like a traditional poodle. So one day, my mom decided to restore some of her dignity by having her groomed to look like the refined gal she was meant to be. When Mom arrived home after Cannoli's shaving, trimming, and pampering, she called us over to see how pretty Cannoli looked. The front door opened and my brothers and I squealed. The dog darted right past us and buried her head—just her head—under the couch, while her well-groomed fanny and cotton-ball tail shivered behind her. We prodded and pleaded, but she wouldn't pull her head out from under the couch.

"She's hiding," Mom explained. "She's embarrassed, and she thinks because she can't see you, you can't see her!"

Sometimes we act a lot like Cannoli. We hide when we're embarrassed—especially when we feel like we've really blown it. We're afraid God is displeased or angry with us, and so we hide because of shame. And in our shame, God feels hidden from us.

Shame is what drove Adam and Eve into hiding from God. They turned away from God's companionship because they had done the one thing he told them not to do:

> Then the man and his wife heard the sound of the LORD God as he was walking in the garden in the cool of the day, and they hid from the LORD God among the trees of the garden. But the LORD God called to the man, "Where are you?"
>
> He answered, "I heard you in the garden, and I was afraid because I was naked; so I hid."

Genesis 3:8–10

Before the catastrophic fruit-eating episode, the couple didn't even know they were naked. But as soon as they bit into the fruit, their eyes were opened and they felt shame. In their nakedness and failure, they felt humiliated. Now, can I just say this? Nakedness is not what they were ashamed of. Nakedness is nothing to be ashamed of. I don't want you to miss the point. They became *aware* they were naked, and so they felt exposed before God. Up to that point, they were unaware and thus felt safe before God. Before their big bite, they were as free as a naked toddler who streaks through the house giggling in front of Mom and Dad—that child has never thought to feel shame or hide. But when Adam and Eve ate the fruit, they tasted disobedience, which brought with it emotions they were never intended to experience. Yet the one thing they did not experience was God's absence. In fact, he was the one walking through the garden calling out, "Adam, where are you?"

To cover our sense of shame, we all try to hide behind some version of the proverbial flimsy fig leaf from time to time. Our fig leaf may be destructive choices, anger toward God, distancing ourselves from our faith or other Christians, or even attempts to perform perfectly for God and others. Whatever we do to try to cover our shame, we do to hide from God. We try to distance ourselves from him because we feel unworthy, embarrassed, or hopeless that we will ever be close to him again. When we choose the shelter of a fig leaf over the shelter of his grace and forgiveness, we can feel like God is so, so far away, even on a distant shore hiding from us. But he isn't, and he won't. God did not hide from Adam in the garden, and he will not hide from you in your shame. He calls to you, as he did to Adam, "Where are you, daughter?" "Where are you, son?" If you are hiding, drop the fig leaf. Come out of hiding, and let God envelop you with his love and forgiveness. He will not condemn you; he only wants to cover you.

Condemnation versus Conviction

Though Adam and Eve were responsible for their choices, it was the enemy of their souls, in the form of a serpent, that set into motion the whole shame-filled cycle of temptation and condemnation. And we have an enemy of our souls too—the same one who tempted Adam and Eve. The Enemy's highest goal is to separate us from God, and shame is one of his most reliable weapons. He is quick to tell us we have blown it and that we are doomed.

Satan's goal is to make you feel ashamed and distant from God. Satan will *condemn* you. In contrast, God's Holy Spirit will *convict* you. Do you know the difference between condemnation and conviction?

Condemnation typically comes in the form of an accusation, like someone else is pointing a finger at you.

- *You blew it.*
- *You are no longer lovable.*
- *God will have nothing to do with you now.*
- *The best thing you can do now is avoid God and hope things eventually work themselves out.*

Conviction, however, tends to come from an inner awareness:

- *I am feeling distant from God.*
- *I have made a bad choice.*
- *I've sinned, and my sin has created a wedge between me and God.*
- *God, please forgive me. I'm sorry. I need to be close to you. I know you are ready to forgive and cover me with your grace.*

Condemnation makes us want to hide and run *from* God; conviction makes us want to come clean and run *to* God. It's important to understand the difference because sometimes it is the deceit of condemnation—rather than the illumination of conviction—that makes us think God is hiding and distant from us. True Holy Spirit conviction will draw you to God. If you feel God is somewhere far away from you, consider whether or not you might be deceived by condemnation. If so, call it what it is, and ask God to convict you and help you address whatever has become a fig leaf separating you from God. Confess it as sin, and allow God to cover you with his forgiveness.

My friend, you have no reason to hide from God, no matter what you have done or how you feel. Don't let your sense of shame separate you from God's presence. He will never be *obvious* to you if you have hidden yourself from him.

The Bible says that "anyone who believes in him will never be put to shame" (Romans 10:11). See, God didn't point a holy finger of condemnation at Adam and Eve. He didn't shake his head in disgust and walk away. No, the Bible says he "clothed them" (Genesis 3:21). If you just realized you are spiritually naked, it's not so

God can shame you; it's so he can clothe you. Let God cover you with his forgiveness and restore you to his companionship. The only kind of hiding you need to do is to be hidden "in the shadow of [his] wings" (Psalm 17:8). I want that sense of peace and safety, don't you?

My sweet, newly groomed puppy hid. She couldn't see us, so she thought we couldn't see her. But I saw her. I was right there. I begged her to come out. Shame, suffering, and sin often make us want to hide or leave us feeling like God is hidden from us. But it is safe to come out, dear one. He sees you. He is with you.

CHAPTER 27

If You Had Been Here

Security is not the absence of danger but the presence of God.

Unknown

When Phil and I were first married, we were in a Walmart one day getting some keys made. We both stood at the counter waiting while the clerk made the duplicates. As we waited, my cell phone rang. I turned slightly away from the counter to take the call. It was my friend Lori, and we chatted for about five minutes. When I hung up, I naturally reached out to put my arm around Phil's waist. As I did, I slipped my hand down and patted him on his—well, you know—we were newlyweds and he had a cute ... well, you know! So I patted his behind, and as I did, I heard him say, "Jennifer, what are you doing?" I could tell he was trying to hold back a laugh. And I could also tell that his voice was not next to me—not attached to the person on whose behind my hand was resting. I was horrified when I realized that his voice was actually behind me! He had stepped away from the counter while I was on the phone, and another man had taken his place.

"Oh my gosh!" I yelped. "I am so sorry, sir!"

By now, Phil was laughing. I didn't have my cane out, and I don't really look blind at first glance, so I'm sure the man had no idea why I had so brazenly patted his backside. I could feel myself turning every shade of red God ever created as the confused and violated man muttered, "No problem," and stepped away.

"Tell him I'm blind," I whispered through clenched teeth. Phil was laughing so hard he couldn't even talk.

"If you had been here, this would not have happened!" I scolded. "Don't walk away from me again. If only you had just been here ... *ugh!*"

Now, I know that is a funny (at least Phil thought it was funny) example of how someone's absence can change everything, but have you ever found yourself thinking, "If God had been here ... ?" We often create if/then scenarios to explain why things happen — or don't happen:

- *If God had been here, the accident wouldn't have happened.*
- *If God had been present, this evil and sorrow wouldn't be going on.*
- *If God had been here, my child would not have died.*

Yet, God is everywhere — omnipresent. So if he is here even when bad things happen, why doesn't his presence protect us and prevent suffering?

If/Then Speculations

You and I are not the first ones to grapple with if/then speculations. The apostle John tells of Martha and her sister Mary, who were heartbroken when their brother Lazarus died. Jesus was a family friend, so they had sent word to him that Lazarus was deathly ill. But Jesus didn't get there until it was too late, and Lazarus died. When Jesus finally arrived, Martha said, "If you had been here, my brother would not have died" (John 11:21).

I love the way she just tells Jesus how it is. And we all get it. We know Martha is saying with her heart, *Lord, I trusted you. Where was your presence when we needed you most?*

Have you ever felt that way? *God, if you had been here, then* _____ *wouldn't have happened? Lord, if your presence was truly with me, this tornado wouldn't have destroyed our home. God, if you really had been with me, how could I have been treated so terribly?*

But consider this — when we engage in if/then speculations, are the assumptions we're making really true? Was Martha's statement to Jesus true? Martha believed Jesus' presence would protect Lazarus from death. She knew he could touch her brother and heal him completely. Jesus had done it for others; he could do it for Lazarus. Therefore, as far as she was concerned, *if* Jesus had been there before Lazarus breathed his last breath, *then* Lazarus would not have died. How did Martha know her assumption was true? Isn't it also possible that Lazarus could have died with Jesus right there with him, holding his hand?

Yes, Lazarus could have died even if Jesus had been there. What happens in our lives has nothing to do with God's *presence* and everything to do with his *providence*. God was right there with my friend Matt as he breathed his last breath. God's presence was right there with my friend Jeannie as her car was crushed by an out-of-control semitruck. God's presence was right there with me when I was declared legally blind. Sometimes we may think it is God's presence that keeps us from hard and awful things. But often it is God's presence that comforts us as he *carries us through* those hard and awful things.

Martha used the word *if* with Jesus after Lazarus died. *If* you had been here, everything would have been OK. She created a perfect past and projected a fantasy future — all with the word *if.*

Martha put that tiny word *if* in a sentence where it just didn't belong. And we do the same thing. We put *if* in our emotional and spiritual vocabulary in places it doesn't belong. *If* is a word of speculation; it is not a word of reality. *If* is not present; *if* is part of a fantasy future or an idealized past we create in our own minds.

How many "ifs" have you placed on God?

When we use the word *if* with God, we are pining for the past or projecting ourselves into the future. We are not present in the now, where God is.

- *If you would just do what you did in the past, I would know you are with me.*
- *If you would just give me a sign for the future, I would know you are with me.*
- *If you would have prevented the accident, I would know you are with me.*
- *If you would make my today just like my yesterday, I wouldn't be so focused on tomorrow, and I could enjoy your presence now.*

If, if, if. It's a never-ending cycle that only makes it more difficult to experience the comfort of God with us right where we are.

Moving from What If to What Is

When we put "ifs" on God, we are not present or attentive to what he is doing in our lives right now. Instead of creating if/then scenarios to satisfy what we don't understand about God's ways, we need to switch our focus from "what if" to "what is." We don't know the "what if"; all we know is the "what is." God *is* with us. God *is* an ever-present help in times of trouble. God *is* sovereign.

Oh, dear friend, if/then scenarios never bring us comfort. We can never know the outcome of our imagined if/thens. We feel, think, and speculate, but we don't know. God's providence is mysterious. Don't create a myth to try to solve the mystery of his ways. Don't try to answer the unanswerable with speculation. When you do, you miss the experience of his presence. Recognize that God is with you. He always has been, and he always will be. It could be he has allowed tragedy in your life for the same reason he allowed Lazarus's death—so you will experience "the glory of God" (John 11:40).

Like me, perhaps you need to let go of some "if/then" statements so you can experience the reality of God's presence with you now. God *is* here, so there is no need to fantasize about the future. Jesus said, "Do not worry about tomorrow, for tomorrow will worry about itself. Each day has enough trouble of its own" (Matthew 6:34). God *is* here, so there is no need to pine for the past. One of the smartest men who ever lived wrote, "Do not say, 'Why were the old days better than these?' For it is not wise to ask such questions" (Ecclesiastes 7:10).

God *is* here, so we can claim his promises as our own: "Never will I leave you; never will I forsake you" (Hebrews 13:5), and "Surely I am with you always, to the very end of the age" (Matthew 28:20). And he didn't use the word *if* at all—so we don't need to either!

CHAPTER 28

Bethel for Your Soul

God doesn't stop crisis from coming, as he didn't stop Christ from coming. Things have their reasons for happening, we need not to faint, but rather have faith that we are never alone.

Anthony Liccione

In September 1850, a group of seven British missionaries set sail for Cape Horn at the tip of South America. They arrived in early December and began their work in harsh conditions on the island of Tierra del Fuego. With provisions for six months, they were expecting that a promised supply ship would bring additional provisions the following spring. But the ship never arrived, and all seven had died of starvation by early September 1851. One of the missionaries was a surgeon named Richard Williams. In his journal he wrote, "Poor and weak though we are, our abode is a very Bethel to our souls, and God we feel and know is here."

Dr. Williams said the place of their starvation was a "Bethel" to them. What an interesting description of a place of barrenness and despair. Do you know the meaning of the word *Bethel*? It comes from the biblical story of Jacob recorded in Genesis 28:10–19.

Jacob's Dream

You remember Jacob, right? The scrappy, not-willing-to-let-go wrestler who took the angel of the Lord to the mat? Jacob was the son of Isaac and grandson of Abraham, which meant he was a pretty important guy. However, as the twin brother of Esau, he was also a guy with a price on his head. Esau had vowed to kill him because Jacob had previously stolen Esau's birthright, the Jewish claim to inheritance and blessing. Years later, as Jacob was on his way to Harran to meet up with family, he stopped to spend the night near Luz. It was an empty field—no hotels, no cot, not even a cave in which to take shelter. He stretched out on the ground and used a stone for his pillow. During the night, he had an amazing dream. You may have heard about his dream, which is often referred to as "Jacob's Ladder."

In the dream, God affirmed for Jacob the promise he had given to Abraham and Isaac: "I am with you and will watch over you wherever you go, and I will bring you back to this land. I will not leave you until I have done what I have promised you" (Genesis 28:15). Jacob was so astounded by the dream that when he woke up, he said, "Surely the LORD is in this place, and I was not aware of it" (Genesis 28:16).

At first glance, a cold, hard plot of land doesn't seem like the kind of place God is likely to show up, but God was there. And could the same be true of your hard place? Is the Lord there, even though you are not aware of it? I believe he is. God is everywhere—with me and with you—and sometimes we just don't recognize it at first.

When Jacob realized he had been visited by God, "He was afraid and said, 'How awesome is this place! This is none other than the *house of God*; this is the gate of heaven'" (Genesis 28:17, emphasis added). The Hebrew words translated as "house of God" are *bayit el*, which can also be transliterated as *beth el*—the word Dr. Williams used in his journal, "Bethel." Think about it—this starving man described the harsh conditions in which he would ultimately lose his life as Bethel, the very house of God.

You know, when things aren't going well for us, when life is hard or uncomfortable, we don't usually say, "How awesome is this place!" Well, maybe you do, but that isn't my first response. Yet, despite the fact that he was running for his life and stuck in an inhospitable place, Jacob didn't hesitate—*awesome* was the only word he could use to describe it.

Jacob was struck with reverence and awe, but let's not forget he had just awakened with a stiff neck and sore back from sleeping on the ground with a rock as his pillow. If you'd just spent the night on hard ground, would you describe that place as awesome?

Oh, not me, sister. Our family recently traveled to China, where Phil was to teach a monthlong course at a university there. It was an unforgettable trip, but there was one thing I would love to forget—the bed. When we entered the hotel room in Dalian, all three of us simultaneously dropped our bags on the floor and plopped onto our beds. That's why there was then a collective cry of pain coming from room 235! Phil, Connor, and I all jumped up as quickly as we had plopped down. The beds were so hard. They felt like boards with a little batting on top. And that wasn't too far from the truth. The beds were actually box springs with sheets on them. No mattresses—just hard boards and rusty coils! None of us have described that hard place as awesome.

But Jacob called his resting place Bethel—not because of the accommodations, but because he knew without a doubt that God was there. Sometimes life's hard places are Bethel to our souls— places that reveal the awesome presence and power of God in completely unexpected ways.

Call It Bethel

When you look back over your life, what hardships would you now call Bethel? Was it a hospital room? A funeral service? A relational loss? What place in your life right now could you call Bethel if you truly believed that God was there with you? Cancer? Infidelity? Unemployment? Infertility? Debt? A hard piece of ground and a rock for a pillow can be a miserable experience, or it can be the discomfort that positions you to experience the presence of God—a very Bethel for your soul.

My friend, I want the hard places in my life to be Bethel, and I know you do too. We don't want to waste the discomfort or pain we experience. We want it to remind us that God is with us rather than reveal we are alone.

So let's be honest. It could be there are times we can't detect God's presence in the barren and hard places because we live independently of him on most days anyway. (It's hard to write that without wincing!) We can't observe or feel his presence when life is as hard as a rock because we don't recognize the astounding reality that he is with us on ordinary days. When suffering comes, it isn't that it removes us from God's presence, but that it reveals we have not relied on his presence all along.

The great Christian theologian Augustine knew what it felt like to finally realize God was there with him, though he had been disinterested or unaware. He wrote, "Too late have I loved you, O Beauty so ancient, O Beauty so new. Too late have I loved you! You were within me but I was outside myself, and there I sought you! In my weakness I ran after the beauty of things you have made. You were with me, and I was not with you."*

Can you relate to Augustine's words? Do you recognize God's presence with you during good and ordinary times? Does what feels like God's absence simply reveal how you haven't noticed his presence all along? If so, my friend, he longs to abide with you. Augustine said it was "too late," but it's not. Just ask Jesus. He said, "Anyone who loves me will obey my teaching. My Father will love them, and we will come to them and make our home with them" (John 14:23).

Jesus wants to make his home with you and make the address of your soul Bethel, the house of God. Invite him in. Ask God to abide with you. He will, my friend.

---

* Augustine, *Confessions*, book 10, chapter 28, www1.villanova.edu/villanova/mission /campusministry/spirituality/resources/spirituality/restlesshearts/prayers.html (accessed July 16, 2013).

CHAPTER 29

He Travels with You on Your Road

I would rather walk with a friend in the dark than walk alone in the light.

Helen Keller

One Sunday morning after church, Phil turned to me and said, "Jennifer, I want you to meet Yakov Smirnoff." Still sitting in the pew, I turned toward Phil and laughed, "Very funny." You see, Phil is ever pulling some kind of prank, usually random and nonsensical. So I admired his imaginativeness in creating this one. Yakov Smirnoff is a Russian-born comedian I had seen on TV years ago. And I still catch his commentaries from time to time on NPR. He always made jokes about the KGB and had a wonderfully distinctive laugh that couldn't be imitated. "Leave me alone," I quipped good-naturedly as I turned back to visit with my friend Joan, who was sitting beside me.

"No, Jennifer, really —" Phil said.

Something in the tone of Phil's voice made me think he might actually be serious. Stranger things have happened, I guess. But still, I wasn't convinced.

"I won't believe it unless I hear him laugh" was my clever retort. Clever, so I thought, until I heard a raspy guffaw that sounded like an asthmatic seal choking up cotton balls. That was the laugh — it was him! There's no mistaking the laugh of Yakov Smirnoff.

I was both embarrassed and charmed. Yakov was funny, engaging, and kind. But who would have thought he'd show up in our church on a Sunday morning? You just never know who is right there with you, do you?

The reality of God's omnipresence is that he is everywhere, but he can reveal himself in ways and in places we least expect—which is just what happened two thousand years ago on a dusty road that stretched between Jerusalem and Emmaus.

The Road to Emmaus

It was the confusing aftermath of Jesus' death and resurrection. Everyone knew he had been crucified, but now reports were circulating that the tomb was empty and some women had actually seen Jesus alive. No one knew what to believe. Devastated by grief and all they had endured, two of Jesus' followers left Jerusalem and headed toward the village of Emmaus, about seven miles from Jerusalem. Depending on their pace, their walk could have taken anywhere from an hour to three hours. As they walked, "they were talking with each other about everything that had happened" (Luke 24:14).

In the midst of their conversation, "Jesus Himself approached and began traveling with them. But their eyes were prevented from recognizing Him" (Luke 24:15–16 NASB). The Greek word translated "approached" is *engizō* (eng-id-zo), which means "to draw near." It is a word that reminds us of the God who once walked in the garden, pursuing Adam and Eve when they were hiding. Now this same God is seeking out two weary, grief-stricken disciples as they try to make sense of their confusion, doubt, and loss. Like his Father, Jesus always gently draws near to us wherever we are. Jesus is Immanuel—God with us. He never barges in or crowds. He simply draws near.

You may be on a difficult road right now. You may feel alone. But Jesus is drawing near to you. Or you may be separated from people you love, and you just can't find peace because you are so concerned about how they must be feeling, so alone and isolated.

Jesus draws near to them too, my friend. He draws near to you, to me, to the ones we love. None of us are ever truly alone.

There is never a moment the Lord is not with us. He walks beside us wherever we walk. He draws near so we will feel his peace and his presence. But just like the two walking buddies on the Emmaus road, we don't always recognize that he is with us. Sometimes we just need to have our spiritual eyes opened to see that what may seem like an ordinary interaction may in fact be a divine interruption.

Divine Interruptions

One of the ways we sometimes affirm God is with us is that he interrupts us! Yes, in the midst of an ordinary day, he interrupts with a splash of divine presence. Sometimes it comes in the form of a warm memory, a glimpse of a beautiful sunset, or a smile or kind word from a stranger. No matter how it comes, a divine interruption is always an expression of Jesus drawing near to us.

On the road to Emmaus, Jesus interrupted the travelers' conversation and asked what they were talking about. One of the disciples named Cleopas just couldn't believe this stranger didn't know about everything that had happened in Jerusalem over the last few days. So he decided to give this ignorant outsider all the details. He described who Jesus was: "He was a prophet, powerful in word and deed before God and all the people" (Luke 24:19). After relating all the tragic events that led to Jesus' crucifixion, Cleopas admitted their disappointment and loss: "We had hoped that he was the one who was going to redeem Israel" (Luke 24:21). Although the disciples had high hopes for Jesus, Cleopas's description reveals that perhaps their hopes weren't high enough—they clearly didn't expect a resurrected Lord.

Do you recognize something of yourself in this story? Like me, do you tend to overlook divine interruptions and then fail to recognize God's presence because you don't expect him to show up? Think about it. Right now, as you read these words, he is with you. His presence is with you. He is Immanuel—God with us.

I have a friend who taught me a lot about what it means to *practice* the presence of God. When I met Lucille, she was in her eighties and had been a widow for about fifteen years. The first time I visited her home for a meal, I noticed that although there were only two of us, she had three place settings on the table. Each placemat had a fork, a knife, and a spoon lying on top of white linen napkins. After she plated our food and set it on the table, she set an empty plate on the third placemat. I finally had to ask.

"Is someone else coming?"

It was like she was waiting for me to ask because she quickly answered, "No, he is already here." She explained that ever since her husband passed away, she intentionally set a place at her table for Jesus. It helped her remember he was with her and helped her feel less alone. Beautiful, isn't it? Lucille expected Jesus to be with her at every meal. That's what it means to practice the presence of God.

The disciples on the Emmaus road didn't expect Jesus, that's for sure. Their forlorn description of what had happened revealed they had no expectation of seeing Jesus again. Their hopes were already dashed.

But these folks had no idea who was walking with them. They didn't fully understand the Scriptures so they didn't clue into the truth that it was Jesus Christ himself with them. You can sense the exasperation in Jesus' response when he says to them, "How foolish you are, and how slow to believe all that the prophets have spoken! Did not the Messiah have to suffer these things and then enter his glory?" (Luke 24:25–26).

Jesus' statement provides a poignant and fascinating insight about why the disciples failed not only to expect Jesus but also to recognize him when he was right there with them. They didn't fully trust the Scriptures. In other words, they were ignorant of God's Word.

Sometimes I think the same thing happens to us. We don't recognize Jesus' presence because we are ignorant of his Word. Let me give you a personal example that demonstrates what I mean.

I have an ordinary looking piece of chipped brick on the bookshelf in my office. It is misshapen, old, and discolored. If you didn't know where it came from, you might easily overlook it. Or if you did notice it, you'd likely disregard it. Why? Because you would be ignorant about the fact that this little piece of brick came from the Kilns—what was once the beloved Oxford home of author C. S. Lewis! Because I am such a devoted Lewis fan, that tiny piece of rock is incredibly valuable to me. If you were a Lewis fan and happened to visit me in my office, wouldn't you be bummed if you missed out on holding that treasured rock simply because you were ignorant of its significance?

That example shows something of what the two travelers on the Emmaus road were experiencing. They were ignorant—not well versed in the biblical truth about the Messiah—so they were clueless about who was walking with them.

Too often, we miss out on experiencing God's presence because we just don't know him. We can't recognize him right there with us because we haven't taken the time or made the effort to really know him by reading his Word. My friend, if you follow Jesus, take the proverbial book off the shelf and get to know him through his Word. Read it, study it, and meditate on it. The Bible reveals who God is. Know it so you will know him.

Even though the disciples weren't aware of Jesus' identity, he was with them—he was walking with them and teaching them. The same applies to you and me. We may not always recognize him, but he is with us. The giggle of a toddler, the gentle rustling of fall leaves scraping the sidewalk, an inspiring cluster of words penned by a master, the sweetness of a strawberry, the strain of a violin or the strum of a guitar—all are reminders that God is with us. He is beauty itself, so any glimpse of beauty that stirs our souls is a reminder that he is with us. God is present in his Word and in our world. Are you paying attention, expecting to see him?

The mystery of the man on the Emmaus road comes to a startling conclusion when "their eyes were opened and they recognized him" (Luke 24:31). Oh, what if those two had missed it? What if they never realized that God incarnate was walking with them? What if their eyes had never been opened? It would break my heart if I found out at the end of my life that God had been walking with me and I had missed out on the joy, security, and peace of that reality. Don't you agree? We need God to open the eyes of our hearts so we can see clearly that he is with us.

You know, I never expected Yakov to be in my church, so I never looked for him. But that has all changed! Ever since my "eyes" were opened to the reality that he was there, I will look for him and expect him to show up again. It's the same with Jesus. Once you realize, even for a moment, that he is with you, you will begin to look for him and expect to see him over and over again. Living with anticipation is one way of having our eyes opened. That's when we begin to live with alertness and eagerness. God expresses his presence to us in so many ways through his creation every minute of every day. He expresses his presence to us through every word of Scripture. We can expect him to be with us — to even surprise us and to always keep pace with our lives.

I don't know what the name of your road is, but I do know that God is with you. On your road, whether it is smooth or rough, Jesus is walking with you.

Expect Jesus to show up in your situation; be sure to look for his interruptions. He will reveal his truth to you through his Word and in your world. Ask God to open your eyes so you, too, can see that the one who walks with you is the one who said, "I am with you always, to the very end of the age" (Matthew 28:20).

You and I may not experience Jesus' physical presence in the same way Cleopas and his walking partner did. After all, they could have reached over and grabbed Jesus' nail-scarred hand if they had wanted to. But we must remember that Jesus is — in a very real and powerful way — just as present with us here today. No matter what you face in your weaknesses, sorrow, fear, or heartache, you are never alone. The writer of the book of Hebrews quotes God's beautiful promise from the Old Testament and applies it to you and me: "Never will I leave you; never will I forsake you" (Hebrews

13:5). That promise, originally written in Hebrew, shows up in the New Testament in Greek. I love how the Greek puts it much more strongly by using five negatives. Literally translated, it would sound something like this: *Never, never, never, never, never will I leave you or forsake you.* And that means, my friend, you are never, never, nope never, not ever, no not ever, ever, never alone!

CHAPTER 30

Keep Walking Toward Him

For every step you take toward God, God takes two steps toward you; and if you come to God walking, God comes to you running.

James Martin, S. J., *In Good Company*

When our family visited Hong Kong, we stopped by the Wong Tai Sin Temple. Of all the places we visited on our trip, this one stands out because of what I heard there. Along with the sounds of birds singing and monks chanting, I heard a constant shaking of sticks. To my ears, it sounded like a bamboo wind chime warehouse that was being attacked by a thousand blow dryers on full blast! I learned from our guide that hundreds of Buddhist worshipers were practicing Kau Cim, or Chinese fortune sticks. It was their way of seeking divine truth and answers to their questions.

In Kau Cim, followers shake long cylindrical tubes filled with flat bamboo sticks that look like incense. Each stick is painted red at one end and has a single, unique number inscribed on it. There are one hundred sticks in each tube. Those seeking divine guidance and answers demonstrate their devotion by kneeling and silently thinking or whispering their question. Then they shake their cylinder, tipping it slightly downward until at least one stick falls out. The number on the stick that falls to the ground corresponds to one of one hundred written oracles. The seekers then have their truth — the answer to the question that is troubling them.

Once I understood what I was hearing and what those precious people were doing, the sound of so much bamboo being shaken was like the sound of so many shaking souls saying, "Tell me, show me, and help me!" And I understood their desperation and their hunger for truth. I've been there, and so have you. We have all asked questions like, *God, are you there?* We all seek truth because we want answers. It is one of the deepest longings of the human heart—especially when life is hard. The hunger for answers is likely why you picked up this book many chapters ago. And that is why I want to introduce you to a woman I've never met.

I'd Like You to Meet the Queen of Sheba

I don't know her, and I'm not even really sure what her name is because she lived thousands of years ago. But if I'd had the honor of knowing her, I think I would really have liked her. Jesus called her the "Queen of the South" (Matthew 12:42). She ruled Sheba, which is the country we call Yemen today. The ancient historian Josephus refers to her as Nicaule, while the Ethiopian people call her Makeda. You and I have heard her called the queen of Sheba. She was born sometime in the tenth century BC.

Here is a bit of her story from the Old Testament: "When the queen of Sheba heard about the fame of Solomon and his relationship to the LORD, she came to test Solomon with hard questions" (1 Kings 10:1). The queen of Sheba was seeking truth and wisdom. Evidently, she'd caught wind of a wise ruler in the north from the travelers who passed through her country. She must have heard traders speak of Solomon's wisdom and decided to investigate the rumors for herself. She wasn't willing to ignore her angst or accept the kind of simplistic answers we find today on refrigerator magnets. She was willing to seek hard and go to great expense in order to learn and discover truth.

Believe it or not, I think you and the queen of Sheba are not very different. You have brought your hard questions to this book, just as the queen brought her search for truth to Solomon. You may have traveled far out of your comfort zone to do so by admitting that sometimes God and faith don't make sense. Or you may be used to seeking, and this is just one more mile along your journey. That's why I like you—you remind me of the queen herself! I love honest seekers who are willing to ask hard questions, willing to learn, willing to be wrong, and willing to persevere until they find truth. And I'm not the only one who feels this way. Jesus himself gave the queen of Sheba the ultimate compliment because he described her as a model seeker. "The Queen of the South will rise at the judgment with this generation and condemn it," he said, "for she came from the ends of the earth to listen to Solomon's wisdom, and now something greater than Solomon is here" (Matthew 12:42). Jesus used the queen of Sheba as an example of how important it is to search for him and to seek the truth. It's an example Jesus encourages us to follow.

Characteristics of the Model Seeker

The queen was a seeker, and she did at least three key things that are worth emulating. Her actions demonstrate what it means not just to seek—wandering aimlessly through the latest religious trends or philosophies—but to seek *truth*, to know "The Truth." So what can we learn from the queen of seekers?

She Was Willing to Leave Her Country in Search of Truth

As a ruling head of state, the queen of Sheba had a whole kingdom to govern. She was the head honcho! She had edicts to give, state dinners to attend, crowns to wear, and government officials to oversee. Her people depended on her. But she left her country for a time to seek out what was most important to her. Think about it. Her identity could have been wrapped up in being the queen. But in leaving her country to seek Solomon's wisdom and his God, she was willing to set aside her identity, to move from being a sovereign to being a seeker.

If you and I really want to experience the fullness of God, especially in our heartaches, we must be willing to let go of our own need for sovereignty, to leave our country, at least for a time, and live like a seeker. That means being willing to admit, "I am not the sovereign of my life. I do not have the wisdom I need to live in the country of my expectations, hopes, and desires. I am not the boss of me. There is one wiser and greater than me. God is the ultimate sovereign in my life, not me."

Setting aside our own sovereignty expresses a queen of Sheba-like choice to seek God's truth above our own need to be the ultimate knower in our lives. Leaving our country is to adopt a queen of Sheba-like willingness to journey through spiritual and emotional discomfort in order to arrive at a place perhaps unfamiliar but incredibly satisfying. To live like a seeker is to have a queen of Sheba-like humility that never assumes we have arrived but is always growing, always on a quest to learn from the Sovereign One who is greater than ourselves.

My friend, you have come to this point in your journey because you have, even within your busy life or heartache, made time to consider and seek truth. In some ways, you have already taken steps to let go of your sovereignty, to leave your country, and to live like a seeker. Way to go! Don't stop. Keep seeking God. The journey is worth it, I promise.

She Didn't Give Up until She Got There

The queen of Sheba traveled a long distance—nearly 3,000 miles round trip—and no doubt incurred a great expense on top of facing hardships and many dangers. Her desire to meet Solomon was so strong that she was willing to take a 1,400-mile journey across the deserts of Arabia, along the coast of the Red Sea, up into Moab, and across the Jordan River to Jerusalem. With the speed limit for most camels at about twenty miles per day, her journey had to have taken at least six months each way. Why did the queen keep traveling, day in and day out, for so long? She kept traveling toward the promise of truth because she valued truth so highly. I don't know about you, but I would have gotten pretty worn-out if I were her. I probably would have questioned at some point if the journey was really worth it. But not her. She was not willing to give up until she reached her destination.

The queen wasn't discouraged by the length or difficulty of her journey. Are we? When we travel through dark valleys in our lives; when we have to endure long and lonely roads, do we get discouraged? When the doctor gives the diagnosis we didn't expect, do we just want to give up on God and try to make it on our own? Do we want to mount our camels and head back to our own countries, where we are sovereign? When the dream we had held so tightly is stripped from our lives, do we decide the journey is no longer worth it? Do we just want to cave in to our discontent or discouragement and give up on God?

When I was in the thick of my journey through depression, boy, did I go through some valleys where I wanted to just give up. I wondered if I would be better off just thinking less and settling for quick answers (even if they weren't the best answers). But my healing came not only in reaching the conclusion of my journey but also in the process of the journey itself. If I had given up or given in, I would not have arrived at the destination of truth and comfort I deeply desired.

When we journey to a place of truth, we often have to journey through places of pain. We encounter sorrow, fear, and a myriad of other emotions that accentuate how hard the journey really is. But the difficult emotions we deal with are what wise seekers endure, knowing they are all part of the process of bringing us to the place of truth and healing.

Are you willing to stay on the journey? Are you willing to meander through the hard places and the hard questions in order to arrive at a place of true peace?

Just because you're near the end of this book, it doesn't mean you've arrived at the end of your seeking; rather, you have your whole life ahead of you to keep walking with and toward God.

Don't let an unexpected heartache or disappointment sidetrack you. Keep asking him your questions and seeking his truth.

She Was Humble and Vulnerable

The brief glimpses we have of the queen of Sheba from Scripture and history portray her as a woman of emotional openness and intellectual curiosity. "She came to Solomon and talked with him about all that she had on her mind. Solomon answered all her questions; nothing was too hard for the king to explain to her" (1 Kings 10:2 – 3). The queen of Sheba showed humility in admitting there were things about God she just didn't understand. The queen was brave enough to make herself vulnerable by sharing what was on her heart, knowing she could have been mocked for her apparent ignorance. But she showed amazing strength in her vulnerability and enviable dignity in her humble willingness to simply be real with Solomon. She left pretense behind in her country. She didn't come to him as a sovereign; she came to him as a seeker. And that is exactly how we should come to God with our questions.

Being a tenderhearted and humble seeker toward God and his truth positions you to be fully satisfied. Are you humble enough to keep asking and seeking? Are you willing to be vulnerable enough before God to admit you don't know or need all the answers? Do you have an open heart? Oh my friend, I hope so. God will never mock or scold you if you ask him questions.

Guard yourself, though, from allowing the questions you ask God to become a substitute for your relationship with God. If you have only an intellectual pursuit of God, all you may end up with is a stale answer. You could become very smart, yet be a discontented genius. But if your heart is open as you seek, you will be willing to receive answers from God, even if you don't like the answers.

The queen (lucky girl) had all her questions answered. "She said to the king, 'The report I heard in my own country about your achievements and your wisdom is true. But I did not believe these things until I came and saw with my own eyes. Indeed, not even half was told me; in wisdom and wealth you have far exceeded the report I heard'" (1 Kings 10:6–7).

The queen didn't settle for hearsay when it came to seeking Solomon's wisdom and his God. She checked it out for herself. I am honored and humbled that you're reading this book. But my friend, don't let this book be "hearsay." Confirm its truthfulness as you meet God face-to-face through his Word and presence. Just as the queen of Sheba saw with her own eyes, come to God with the eyes of your own heart. Keep coming to God, and let him prove to you that he is bigger, wiser, and more satisfying than you could have ever imagined.

Be willing to seek, but also be willing to humbly accept the answers God gives—or chooses not to give. We may not always get all the answers we want from God, but we get something far better. We receive a relationship with God himself.

The Journey Ahead

Together, you and I have taken steps throughout the pages of this book to find answers to the tough questions of faith. We have asked, "God, do you care?"; "God, are you there?"; and "God, are you fair?" among others. We ask the questions because they really do matter.

The queen of Sheba undertook a great journey to find truth and meaning. You and I also have a long road to travel in this life. But only two steps really matter most, which are the two steps we take in our heart each day—one step out of demanding our own sovereignty, and one step into trusting God's.

The queen of Sheba would tell you and me to keep seeking the God of all wisdom. Never stop seeking; never stop walking with and toward him. Jesus invites us to keep taking steps toward him, even if every stepping-stone is in the shape of a question mark. As you continue to seek, don't let theological information become a substitute for faith. Don't let knowledge become a substitute for wisdom. And don't seek God only for the answers he gives—seek God himself. Pursue an encounter with the God who loves you. Don't settle for mere answers, my friend. Be satisfied with nothing less than God himself.

CONCLUSION

What I Really Want
You to Know

Never be afraid to trust an unknown future to a known God.

Corrie ten Boom

Psychiatrist and Holocaust survivor Viktor Frankl wrote that suffering without meaning leads to despair. And he's right. Without meaning, there is certain to be despair. But sometimes we assume that meaning is only revealed by understanding. In other words, if something makes sense to me, *then* I can find meaning in it. But meaning can also exist in the absence of understanding, even if the *why* of our circumstances is never answered. The reason there is meaning is because of the *Who*. Standing at the center of every unanswered question is the person of God, who is your provision even in the midst of mystery.

Admitting we don't understand all the ways of God isn't the same as admitting defeat. Instead, it's an admission of our fragile and limited humanity. It's also an admission that comes with a gift. It frees us to relax in the unknown and revel in the mystery. Instead of resisting God's ways, we can simply rest in them. That's when we settle into the security of God's sovereignty. It takes a lot of emotional and mental energy to unscrew that which is intentionally inscrutable. Scripture reveals that "the secret things belong to the LORD our God" (Deuteronomy 29:29). There are simply supposed to be things about God we do not and will never understand.

But we are to trust in the Lord with all our hearts, not relying on our own understanding (Proverbs 3:5). In other words, we don't have to understand everything about God to trust him fully.

God does not always remove question marks, but he does punctuate our lives with meaning, even in the mystery. A hard path can still be meaningful because of the encounter we have with God within and because of the mystery itself.

We are all on different places along the road of faith. Some of us have gotten lost and become distracted by detours because the questions are too many and the answers are too few. Others of us are contentedly cruising along because trusting what we don't understand about God isn't too hard for us most of the time. Where you are on the road is not nearly as important as the fact that you are on the road. The queen of Sheba did not allow herself to get sidetracked or to turn away from finding the truth she sought. That is what I want for you and me too. Determine to stay on your road, my friend. Bumpy or smooth, curvy or straight—stay on the road of faith. I have decided to journey on, and that one decision makes every injury hurt less and every question feel less threatening.

As you keep walking and seeking, if you find yourself smack-dab in the middle of a hard place on your road of faith, I want you to remember three things:

1. Every struggle is a snapshot. What you struggle with—whether it's debt, disease, grief, or any other number of difficulties—is not the whole picture. It's just one snapshot in the whole photo album that is your life. It is not forever. Eventually, life's pages will turn. Sure, this hard place will always be a part of you, but eventually, it will not be the biggest part of you. Just like an old photo in an album, the pain will become a faded memory. And if your struggle is something like a life-threatening cancer, even that awful circumstance isn't permanent. In light of eternity, even what is terminal is temporary. If you're living with a disability or chronic disease, you may think every page of your life features the same snapshot. Each day is a picture of pain, loss, and struggle. But even what is chronic will eventually cease. Even if it doesn't cease until the day your body passes from death to life, it *will* go away. Keep your pain in perspective—eternal perspective.

2. Every trial can be a teacher. Your struggles may cause you to experience loss, but you can also gain wisdom and deeper understanding if you allow them to teach you. I learned many years ago that it was counterproductive to fight against what God had allowed—namely, blindness. I gain far more from the loss by asking it to be my friend and my teacher. At this point in my life, I expect blindness to give more than it takes from me. I have received wisdom and greater faith because I have been willing to learn from my blindness.

What about your situation? Are you willing to submit to it as your teacher? Think about the knowledge you have found in your unanswered questions. What foolishness can you leave behind because of what you will learn from it? Suffering may be a demanding schoolmaster, but you will graduate with a wisdom you can't often learn anywhere else. So be a diligent student, my friend.

3. Every mystery of faith can become a ministry. Every struggle contains an opportunity for you to redeem your loss by reaching out to others. Did you know, for example, that the apostle Paul wrote significant portions of the New Testament—Colossians, Philemon, Ephesians, Philippians—while he was in prison in Rome? He could have seen incarceration as lost time or have fallen into self-pity. Paul could have legitimately indulged in resisting his circumstances by refusing to let go of asking, "Why, God?" He could have spent his days crying out, "God, are you fair? God, are you aware of me in this prison?"

Some people spend their whole lives asking questions like, "God, do you hear prayer?" "God, are you there?" "God, are you aware?" But what if you take those same kinds of questions and reverse them: "Do *I* care? Am *I* there for others? Am *I* aware of the pain around me? Am *I* an answer to the prayers of others?" When we become part of the answer for others who suffer, the questions concerning our own suffering seem to take on greater meaning and, at the same time, diminish in significance.

Dear friend, it can feel like the things of this earth are permanent, but they aren't. They are just a snapshot, a screen capture, a blurry and imperfect image of a bunch of pieces loosely knit together by our hopes, plans, and circumstances. And even when those pieces are broken or missing, they can still teach us and become a source of ministry. The empty, ugly, and hard places in life can actually become the places where we find the real peace we long for because God is there.

Every difficult, confusing season in life offers a choice. You can either surrender your questions and sorrow to God so he can use them, or you can surrender to bitterness and the enemy of your soul, who will use them against you. Don't give him the weapons to hurt you. Trust God, be patient, and even forgive him if you need to. Humble yourself and wrap yourself in your blanket of faith. In doing so, you will turn your sorrow into a tool that refines you and makes you beautiful. In doing so, you will find meaning in your sorrow.

Well, that's what I really wanted you to know. So, until heaven...

Bless you, my friend,
Jennifer

Threads of Truth for Your Blanket of Faith

- For the LORD will not abandon His people, nor will He forsake His inheritance. (Psalm 94:14 NASB)
- "I will be with you as I was with Moses. I will not fail you or abandon you." (Joshua 1:5 NLT)
- The LORD is close to the brokenhearted; he rescues those whose spirits are crushed. The righteous person faces many troubles, but the LORD comes to the rescue each time. (Psalm 34:18–19 NLT)
- "The LORD your God goes with you; he will never leave you nor forsake you." (Deuteronomy 31:6)
- "Do not fear, for I am with you; do not be dismayed, for I am your God. I will strengthen you and help you; I will uphold you with my righteous right hand." (Isaiah 41:10)

Visit jenniferrothschild.com/threads to download free Scripture cards.

Acknowledgments

Julie White: I don't think Zondervan would have accepted this book if it had not first passed through your wise tweaking. People have no idea how bad a blind woman's manuscript can look before someone sighted and compassionate gets hold of it! Thanks for being my first reader and fixer.

Christine Anderson: What a wonderful editor! You were just what this book and this author needed. I love that you are smarter than I am! Thanks for your thorough and grace-filled editing.

Carolyn McCready: Thank you for being someone I can trust as a friend and a professional. And thanks for letting me follow you around! I am so grateful for you.

Phil: In my iPhone contacts I have you identified as "Stud Husband." Enough said! I love you. Thanks for being my manager and best friend.

C. S. Lewis: I know he's long since passed, but I still must acknowledge him. God used him as an authoritative guide who helped me feel safe asking the questions in this book. He walked with me through many doubts and dark days of depression. I am so deeply grateful for this wise Christian brother. After Jesus, he is the first person I want to meet in heaven. I think we will have coffee together for about the first thousand years. Well, I'll have coffee; I think he is a tea drinker!